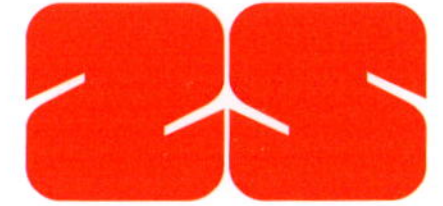

ISBN 978-3-89883-196-3

Photography
Recipes: Susie Eising
Spreads and portraits: Alexander Haselhoff (s.a. picture credits)

Foodstyling: Monika Schuster
Recipe support: Monika Reiter, Gerlinde Reiter, Patrick Raaß
Graphic design: Georg Feigl
Illustrations: Johann Brandstetter
Editors: Gertrud Köhn, Edelgard Prinz-Korte, Alexandra Schlinz
Translation: Editorial Office Weinberger, Munich (Renate Weinberger, Joyce Henderson, Ina Stockhousen)
Editorial assistant: Martin Kintrup
Production: Karin Mayer, Peter Karg-Cordes
Lithography: Christine Rühmer

Printing and binding: L.E.G.O., Vicenza
Printed in Italy

In cooperation with Bayerisches Fernsehen (BR), Munich

Please visit our website: www.zsverlag.de

ALFONS SCHUHBECK

MY BAVARIAN COOKBOOK

Contents

My Bavarian Cooking

Bavarian cooking has a long and magnificent tradition. It is solid and rustic, honest and uncomplicated, whereby it can be fine and distinctly sophisticated. It has allowed itself to be somewhat influenced by Austrian and Swabian flavors, as well as South Tyrol's cuisine, which I have found most inspiring.

When I was young, I wanted to explore the world. I cooked my way from Salzburg to Geneva, from Paris to London; and do not forget, of course I cooked in Munich. There, the renowned chef Eckart Witzigmann introduced me to haute

cuisine. During my year of apprenticeship and years of travel, I watched, learned, and tried out many things. A good cook has to continue to experiment and make discoveries. Then, I found my luck in my Bavarian homeland at a beautiful place called Waging. There, I cooked with natural and organic products from the region. Good meat only comes from healthy animals and good vegetables have to be grown in good soil. That is my opinion and I have continued to cook according to this principle until today, and at the "Platzl" in Munich as well. I haven't reinvented Bavarian cooking, but I have changed it. I have made it a little bit lighter, much more variable, and perhaps even a bit brighter. Spices have turned out to have a big influence in my cooking and give my dishes more character and digestibility.
My first Bavarian cookbook was published in 1989, and meanwhile, has come out in 18 editions. I have worked a long time on this new book, integrating my accumulated knowledge of cooking with the desire to respond to the changes in modern cuisine. It is my most in-depth and final answer to the subject: "My Bavarian cookbook". I hope that this book will have a special place in your kitchen, and that your style of cooking will be inspired again. So grab your spoon and let's get down to cooking. Here we go!

Alfons Schuhbeck is an offspring from his native land. His style of cooking is not only the result of what shaped and influenced him while growing up. The natural beauty of the Bavarian countryside gives him energy and inspiration for his culinary creations.

A Truly Devoted Cook

A good catch! The fisher presents proudly, the catch of the day. Alfons Schuhbeck knows: freshness guarantees quality.

When a person hangs on to something that is conventional, then he is conservative. Whereas, when he revises or modifies something that is already there, or at least tries to, he is called a revolutionary. Whoever would like to put Alfons Schuhbeck in one of these two pigeonholes will fail. Instead, he will discover that he is dealing with a conservative revolutionary. This man from the Chiemgau area is different than most of his professional colleagues. Why? Whereby, it is not a question of whether he is better or worse than other cooks. It is rather a question of "how". What is he like, and how does he cook?

At the beginning of his life as a cooking artist, his regular guests at "Kurhausstüberls" in Waging at Waginger See, which he managed, considered him to be an "up front type of person". The things that the born Traunsteiner accomplishes in the kitchen are also done in a straightforward way.

The "Magician of Bavarian Cooking", as one of his fans calls him, moved to Munich in 2003. The move was the result of his "insatiable quest to repeatedly take on something new". Already in his younger years, Alfons discovered that becoming a cook is hard work. Of his travels through a succession of very highly praised kitchens, he says: "I kept my eyes and ears wide open all the time." His willingness to assimilate something new, different and better has born fruit, since he has been professionally independent. Therefore, after his return from his travels on the road through Austria, Switzerland, France, Great Britain, and Germany, he instinctively understood that many people come to value homemade meals prepared with regional ingredients. Moreover, dishes needed to be lighter and more easily digestible. With that in mind, he continued to experiment, until his dishes were not only a delight to the palate but light and easily digested. In the course of the years, his recipes would be duplicated all over Germany.

Alfons Schubbeck prefers to take care of the selection of the products himself. Smelling, tasting, feeling – that is a sensual enjoyment for him.

Today, even North Germans think highly of Obatzda or Topfenpflanzerl with green salad. They like potato cheese, Bavarian Coleslaw, jellied cured meat from Bavarian cockerel, fried char, Weisswurstradel (Bavarian white sausage wheels) on lentil salad just as the Bavarians do. They take pleasure in eating Hendl (chicken) soup, sweet chestnut soup with truffle or sweet-sour marinated rostbratwurst. They ask for another serving of Noodle Gangerl or Schlutzkrapfen. They want Steckerlfish with potato-cucumber salad, and wels catfish steamed in vegetable stock. They say "yes" to grilled roast suckling pig, Böfflamott, and

Good quality is close at hand. That's why it is a matter of the heart for Alfons Schuhbeck to cook with regional ingredients from his Bavarian homeland.

to medium roasted beef tenderloin with cardamom butter. Thanks to Schuhbeck, many hobby cooks are now acquainted with the most diverse ways to prepare Knödel (dumplings). Then there's Mehlspeise (pastries, batter pudding): especially Strudel, Buchteln, and all kinds of Kucherl and other local specialty. Thanks to Alfons Schuhbeck, the menu in many homes has become more diversified, multifarious, and more Bavarian.

Today, it is indeed justified to say: Schuhbeck, who is highly decorated for his cooking skills, is one of the best-known cooks in Germany. His way of working has long since gained acceptance far outside of Bavaria's borders. His appeals to not only pay attention to the quality of the food that is used, but moreover, to handle it with great care, is meanwhile not only being observed in the Free State of Bavaria. His advice to "turn down the heat" has gained popularity even among professionals. He has taught his female and male colleagues, many housewives and male cooking amateurs: Meat and fish need time – their own time – to cook. Meat "relaxes", when it is allowed to cook gently.

When Alfons Schuhbeck started sharing his knowledge and findings, his understanding and opinions, he declared: "To minimize loss of fragrance and flavor, fresh herbs, which round off and enhance every meal, should be prepared and added just before serving." Over the years, Schuhbeck has complemented his knowledge regarding the use and care of aromatic plants from garden and fields with an in depth "know-how" on the subject of exotic spices. He has mastered the art of turning a

simple dish into a gourmet sensation through his innovative addition of herbs and spices. To reduce the loss of potency, fragrance, and aroma of spices, he considers it important that they aren't added too early in the cooking process. Hence, timing and having a feel for the ideal quantity make all the difference. According to Alfons Schuhbeck these two qualities distinguish a good cook from an average one. The stories he can tell about anise, chili, fennel, cloves, ginger, cardamom, garlic, coriander, cumin, curcuma (also turmeric), bay leaves, mace, nutmeg, the different types of pepper, allspice, saffron, mustard seeds, vanilla pods, juniper berries, and cinnamon are absolutely fascinating. However, most importantly, Schuhbeck underlines that he does not only use herbs and spices to vary the taste of a dish but to add nutritional value to every meal.

Alfons Schuhbeck loves to be outdoors. Here he has the rare opportunity to do nothing but relax.

Moreover, for that, what the Germans put on table, he preaches unremittingly like a missionary. He advocates relentlessly that cleanliness and using only the freshest ingredients are of utmost importance. Therefore, when it comes to shopping, less is more. For meat, he explains: it has to ripen occasionally up to fourteen days and wait for its preparation. But above all, the golden rule for those who want to make themselves and others happy with a good meal is to take the following principle to heart: The art of cooking requires devotion and patience, patience and still more patience.Typical for a conservative revolutionary.

Food

Herbs

Herbs like **parsley, chives, chervil, basil, dill, bear's garlic, sorrel, or watercress** are best preserved if they are rinsed briefly under cold water. After gently shaking off excess moisture, they are wrapped in a damp paper towel and then stored in the refrigerator in a well-closed container or wrapped up in plastic wrap. The leaves should be plucked from the stalks first as needed and cut only into small pieces. The aroma suffers if they are chopped too fine. Once cut, herbs have to be used quickly to maintain their full aroma. Since their essential oils evaporate quickly, they could end up smelling like hay if not used within 20 or 30 minutes.

Whoever would like to always have a supply of fresh herbs handy has the choice of freezing those mentioned above. After cutting it is the best to spread them out on a plate stretched with a plastic wrap and then cover with plastic wrap. As soon as the herbs are frozen, they can be placed in a freezer container and used as needed.

Some herbs like **marjoram, savory, or oregano** unfold their aroma, when they are dried. Kept in a well-closed jar, they are available any time.

Freshly cut herbs should be added to dishes shortly before serving the meal. However, dried marjoram, savory, or oregano should be added just two to three minutes before the end of cooking time, so that the aroma has time to unfold.

Because of their strong individual taste, I usually use **thyme, rosemary**, marjoram, savory, and oregano by themselves rather than in combination with other herbs. Mild herbs like **parsley or chervil** are an exception. The chopped leaves from thyme and the needles from rosemary can be used for mixtures to cook au gratin. But usually, one tends to lay these herbs as sprigs in a dish at the end of the cooking time for about five minutes and then takes them out again.

Parsley**, dill, tarragon or basil** can also flavor dishes, if they are allowed to steep a few minutes before removal. Finally, I use parsley stalks for flavoring when heating up Bavarian white sausages (the famous Bavarian special called Weisswurst).

Spices

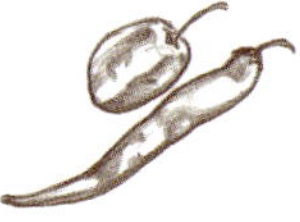

Dried spices that are stored dry, protected from light, and in an airtight container, keep for about two years. If they are not cut up into small pieces, they keep longer. One can produce an individual spice blend from several spices like **pepper, allspice, juniper berries, cinnamon, chili, coriander, and bay leaves**. Fill everything into a spice grinder to grind as needed. For freshly ground pepper, I use black peppercorns or mix it with other types of pepper like green pepper. **Ground spices** should be added during the last minutes of the cooking time because they develop their flavor very quickly. With meat or fish dishes, rather than putting the spices directly onto the product, I prefer to stir them into the soup or sauce at the end. Another option is to add them to melted butter or, even better, slightly warmed oil and drizzle the mixture over the cooked products. When using whole dried spices in cooking, it's the best to put them in a small spice bag, for instance, a one-way tea bag closed with a clip.

Fresh **garlic and ginger** are also added to a dish at the end. When using garlic, I like to cut it in half or slices, which makes it easy to remove a few minutes later and facilitates pinpointing the desired dosage and flavor. I also use sliced ginger (peeled or unpeeled). The combination of ginger and garlic provides a more delicate flavor. Ginger has the added bonus of masking the strong garlic odor.

Strips from **citrus fruit peel** make for a fresh touch in dishes; because of its sourness, the juice is often not suitable for flavoring. If organic (untreated) fruit is unavailable, rub off the wax layer well, using hot vinegar water or hard liquor. **Vanilla** is excellent for rounding off sweet as well as hearty dishes. It blends well with garlic, giving a more refined and milder taste. To use the vanilla pod, bisect it lengthwise and then scrape out the seeds with the edge of the knife and add, for instance, to Bavarian cream. To make vanilla sugar, add the scraped pods to sugar and store in a suitable container. Or let the scraped pods steep in cherry compote, vanilla sauce and the like as well as in hearty dishes for a few minutes at the end of cooking time.

Oils & Butter

Because of its high smoking temperature refined vegetable oils are suitable for searing and browning fish or meat. High temperature cooking decomposes fats. After frying, excess oil should be removed from food with absorbent paper. Cold pressed oils like **olive, canola, sunflower, argan, and pumpkin seed oil** offer high nutritional value, and are ideally used for cold dishes like salads. Warm dishes are best sprinkled with a few drops after preparation.

To aromatize oils, choose a mild cold-pressed oil. Spices and oil are gently warmed for a few minutes, allowing the aroma to be absorbed quickly without compromising nutritional values. The following spices are suitable: Rosemary, thyme, chili peppers, garlic, ginger, lemon peel, cardamom and vanilla. For citrus oils, grate some peel of the desired citrus fruit in cold olive oil, the aroma will unfold immediately.

I apply flavorful argan oil with a basting brush just before serving (for instance, on a beef filet steak). I combine pumpkin seed and nut oil with more mellow oils; they are too overpowering on their own. Truffle oil has an intense flavor, so it is only used in drops to perfume. Cold-pressed oils maintain their quality for eight to twelf months at room temperature, and noticeably longer in the refrigerator. They do flocculate at lower temperatures, but become clear again when returned to room temperature. The best way to store truffle oil is frozen in a bottle. When needed, run warm water over the bottle, withdraw the desired amount, and freeze the rest again.

Butter has a lower smoking and burning point than oil and should only be used at moderate temperatures. It is suitable for the browning of batter pudding resp. pastries (in German called Mehlspeisen), for instance, pancakes, and for the gentle braise of vegetables. Its delicate flavor comes best into play, when mixed into soups or sauces just before serving. Butter creates a cohesive consistency, making soups and sauces smooth and creamy. For best results, it has to be added cold.

For **flavoring butter,** I melt the butter at low heat, and add spices like garlic, vanilla beans, ginger, and lemon zests and finish seasoning with salt and pepper. A light coating of the mixture enhances fried meat or chicken breast. Clarified butter is made by melting butter over moderate heat. The froth is skimmed from the surface and discarded. The butter is cooked until all of the water has evaporated. Clarified butter, kept in an airtight container in the refrigerator, can be stored for several months. Clarified butter will not burn at high temperatures and is suitable for browning breaded dishes like Viennese Schnitzel.

Brown butter is also called nut butter because of its nutty taste. It keeps at least eight weeks in the refrigerator. When cold, it becomes hard, when needed it is warmed up and used for seasoning vegetables and batter puddings. It can be drizzled over asparagus and pasta. Combined with garlic and vanilla pods it tastes nice as a flavoring for fried fish.

Seasoning & Flavoring

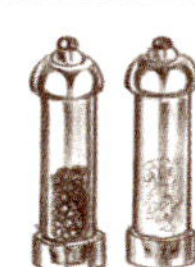

With a few exceptions – for instance, vacuum-poached articles – I add **salt** only at the end of the cooking time, so that the food remains juicier. If salt is added in the beginning, then meat juices escape unnecessarily during the cooking process. This is particularly noticeable with dishes consisting of thinly sliced meat or mushrooms, but also with pan-fried pieces. If you choose to season or flavor towards the end of cooking time; everything taste more flavored.

Whole **spices** are added directly to soups or sauces and then removed again. For fish and meat, melt butter or warm up the oil of your choice, infuse with the chosen spices, season with salt and pepper and coat the finished fried products with the mixture. To season, I use strips or (grated) zest from citrus fruit peels (zest is the outer colorful skin of citrus fruits, in kitchen lingo it means also gratetd zest). For strips from organic (untreated) fruits like lemons or oranges, it is best to peel off the fruit with a potato peeler. To obtain grated zest rub off the peels with a zester grater. You can take the strips out of the dish very easily. For some dishes like burgers, grated zest is more suitable than strips.

Snacks & Starters

Farmer's Omelet with Ham

14 oz (400 g) low starch potatoes
salt
1 onion
3.5 oz (100 g) cooked ham
3 oz (80 g) wide green beans
1 carrot
5 oz (150 g) broccoli
3.5 oz (100 g) cocktail tomatoes
1 tbsp oil
freshly ground pepper
cayenne pepper
dried savory
1 tbsp freshly chopped parsley leaves
1/2 garlic clove, chopped
5 eggs
5/8 cup (150 ml) milk
freshly grated nutmeg
3 oz (80 g) grated cheese, e.g. white cheddar or Monterey Jack

4 servings

1 Peel the potatoes, wash and cut into 0.2 inch (5 mm) thick slices. Cook in a large quantity of salted water for 15 to 20 minutes. Pour into a sieve and cool off.

2 Peel and finely dice onion. Cut ham into small cubes. Clean beans, wash and cut them diagonally in 0.6 inch (1.5 cm) wide pieces. Clean the carrot, peel and cut into slices. Clean broccoli, wash and separate into small flowerets. Blanch beans, carrot, and broccoli separately in boiling salted water firm to the bite. Remove with a skimmer, rinse off with cold water and drain. Wash the cocktail tomatoes and cut in half.

3 Heat the oven to 350 °F (180 °C). Heat the oil in an ovenproof skillet. Fry potatoes and onions over medium heat until golden brown. Add ham, beans, carrots, broccoli and cocktail tomatoes. Season with some salt and pepper as well as a pinch of cayenne pepper and savory. Add parsley and garlic.

4 Beat eggs and milk in a tall bowl with a wand mixer. Season the egg-milk mixture with some nutmeg, salt, pepper and cayenne pepper and spread over the vegetables. Leave the skillet another 30 seconds on top of the stove, and then cook in the oven on the middle rack for about 20 minutes.

5 After 15 minutes cooking time, spread grated cheese over the farmer's omelet. To serve, invert the omelet from the skillet onto a platter and cut into pieces.

Alfons Schuhbeck

"To invert the omelet easily from the skillet onto a plate, it is best to use a non-stick skillet. Protect the pan handle in the hot oven by covering it with aluminum foil."

SAUSAGE SALAD

For the marinade:

3 shallots
1 kohlrabi
2 small carrots
6 stalks green asparagus
3 oz (80 g) green beans
salt
2 tsp icing sugar
1 1/4 cups (300 ml) vegetable stock
1 tsp hot mustard
1–2 tbsp red wine vinegar
2 tbsp mild olive oil
1 tsp walnut oil
1 slice each of garlic and ginger
freshly ground pepper
cayenne pepper
sugar
1 tbsp freshly chopped parsley leaves

Additional ingredients:

1.7 lb (800 g) Regensburg sausages
1 tbsp freshly chopped parsley leaves

4 servings

1 For the marinade: Peel shallots and cut into thin rings. Clean and cut kohlrabi and carrots. Cut kohlrabi into eight pieces and crosswise into 0.1 inch (3 mm) thin slices. Cut carrots diagonally into 0.1 inch (3 mm) thin slices. Wash asparagus, peel only the lower third of the stalks and remove the stringy ends. Cut the asparagus stalks diagonally into 1.2 to 2 inches (3 to 5 cm) long pieces. Clean and wash beans, cut into 0.8 inch (2 cm) long pieces and blanch in salted water for 5 to 6 minutes. Pour the beans into a sieve, rinse off with cold water and drain.

2 Caramelize the icing sugar in a saucepan over medium heat. Add shallots, kohlrabi, carrots and asparagus, and braise lightly over medium heat. Pour the stock on top, and cook the vegetables for about 10 minutes until firm to the bite. Pour into a sieve and collect the broth in a dish. Let vegetables cool off a bit. Then mix with beans in a bowl.

3 Measure off half of the stock and stir in mustard, vinegar and both types of oil. Let garlic and ginger infuse the marinade for a few minutes and remove again. Season the marinade until spicy with salt and pepper as well as a pinch of cayenne pepper and sugar. Stir in parsley.

4 To serve, peel skin off the Regensburg sausages and cut sausages into 0.1 to 0.2 inch (3 to 5 mm) thick slices. Fold the sausage slices together with parsley into the vegetables. Pour the marinade on top and mix well all ingredients. Season the sausage salad to taste and serve in a bowl or in a deep dish.

"Instead of Regensburg sausages – in German called Regensburger Würste –, you can use other type of sausages like Wienerwurst or Lyoner (fine ring bologna). Shallots can be substituted with red onions."

OBATZDA WITH PEARS AND CROUTONS

For the croutons:

2 slices white bread
3 tbsp butter
2 tbsp oil

For the Obatzda (spicy cheese mix):

1/2 ripe firm pear
5 green onions
9 oz (250 g) ripe Camembert (room temperature)
9 oz (250 g) cream cheese
3–4 tbsp cream
2 tbsp Williams Pear brandy
salt
cayenne pepper
ground caraway seeds
brown butter (see page 26)

4 servings

1 For the croutons: Remove the crust from the white bread and cut bread slices with a sharp knife once more lengthwise. Cut the bread slices into 0.2 inch (5 mm) thin strips and then into smallest possible cubes. Heat butter and oil in a skillet and brown the bread cubes over medium heat until light brown. Drain on paper towel.

2 For the Obatzda: Peel pear, core and dice finely. Clean, wash and cut the green onions into thin slices.

3 Cut the Camembert into small pieces and stir in a bowl with cream cheese, cream and Williams Pear brandy until creamy. Fold in pear cubes and green onions. Season the Obatzda with salt, a pinch each of cayenne pepper and caraway seeds, and some brown butter.

4 To serve, fill a bowl with the Obatzda and spread croutons on top. According to taste, serve with radishes, bread, pretzels or whole grain rolls.

"It is easier to cut the bread into small pieces if the bread slices are somewhat frozen."

Potato Cheese

14 oz (400 g) low starch potatoes
salt · 1/2 tsp caraway seeds
1 onion · 2 tbsp butter
1 tbsp each of coriander corns, caraway seeds and black peppercorns
7 fl oz (200 g) sour cream
4 tbsp brown butter (see page 26)
cayenne pepper
dried marjoram
freshly grated nutmeg
2 tbsp finely chopped chives

4 servings

1 Wash potatoes and boil in a large saucepan with salted water and caraway seeds for 15 to 20 minutes until tender. Pour off the water and peel potatoes as hot as possible. Mash in a bowl with a potato masher.

2 Peel and finely dice onion. Melt the butter in a skillet and brown the onion cubes over low heat until light brown on all sides. Fill a spice grinder with coriander corns, caraway seeds and peppercorns.

3 Add onion cubes, sour cream and brown butter to the potatoes in the bowl and mix well. Season the potato-cheese mixture with salt and a pinch each of cayenne pepper, marjoram, nutmeg and the mixture from the spice grinder. Finally, stir chives into the sandwich spread. This type of sandwich spread – in German called Kartoffelkäs – tastes best on coarse brown bread.

Goats' Topfen Mixed with Apricots

1 small red onion
7 dried, soft apricots
2 tbsp sunflower seeds
12 oz (350 g) goats' curd cheese (quark) or as an alternative: 9 oz (250 g) cream quark stirred with 3.5 oz (100 g) goat cream cheese
3–3.5 fl oz (80–100 g) cream
2 tbsp melted butter
1 tbsp acacia honey
salt · cayenne pepper
2 tbsp finely chopped chives

4 servings

1 Peel and finely dice onion. Cut apricots in half and then into small cubes. Gently toast the sunflower seeds in a non-stick skillet without fat over low heat and cool off.

2 Stir the curd cheese with cream, melted butter and honey until smooth. If the curd cheese is very dry, add some cream. Season with salt and cayenne pepper. Fold onion and apricot cubes with chives into the cheese mixture and season once more. Pour the cheese mixture into a bowl and sprinkle with sunflower seeds.

3 This sandwich spread is excellent with hearty coarse brown bread or whole grain bread.

"In Bavaria, Topfen is a special sort of curd cheese. Instead of sunflower seeds, sprinkle the quark mixture with chopped walnuts or small croutons, which have been fried in butter."

TOPFENPFLANZERL WITH GREEN SALAD

For the Topfenpflanzerl (burgers made from quark):

7 oz (200 g) Alpine Cheese or as an alternative: Monterey Jack
3 oz (80 g) white bread
2 tbsp milk
1.7 lb (800 g) quark (curd cheese)
1/2 onion · 5 tbsp oil
1 tsp each of fennel and caraway seeds, coriander corns and black peppercorns
2 egg yolks
1 tbsp brown butter (see page 26)
1/2 tsp grated organic lemon zest
1 tbsp freshly chopped parsley leaves
salt
1/2 tsp each of ground turmeric and sweet paprika powder
freshly grated nutmeg
cayenne pepper
1 cup (100 g) white bread crumbs

For the salad:

12 oz (350 g) mixed green salad
1/3 cup (80 ml) vegetable stock
2 tbsp currant vinegar
1 tsp hot mustard
2 tbsp mild olive oil
salt · sugar
cayenne pepper

4 servings

1 For the Topfenpflanzerl: Remove the crust from the cheese and cut into 0.1 to 0.2 inch (3 to 4 mm) cubes or shred the cheese with a grater. Take the crust off the white bread and cut the bread into small cubes. Place bread cubes in a bowl and sprinkle with drops of milk. Place quark in a wet cheese cloth and press out the liquid forcefully so that only about 14 ounces (400 g) dry quark (Topfen) remain.

2 Peel and finely dice onion. Heat a tablespoon oil in a skillet and braise the onion cubes over low heat until translucent. Fill the spice grinder with fennel and caraway seeds as well as coriander and peppercorns.

3 Add the dry quark to the white bread in the bowl and mix with cheese cubes, egg yolks, onion cubes, brown butter, lemon zest and parsley. Season the quark mixture with salt, turmeric, paprika, nutmeg, a pinch of cayenne pepper and the mixture from the spice grinder.

4 Spread white bread crumbs on a plate. Shape the quark mixture with wet hands into small Topfenpflanzerl (burgers) and turn them in the white bread crumbs.

5 Heat the remaining oil in a skillet and fry the Topfenpflanzerl over low heat slowly on both sides. Drain on paper towel. (If burgers are fried too fast, then they should be cooked several minutes longer in an oven preheated to 350 °F [175 °C] until they are well done.)

6 For the salad: Clean green salad, wash, spin dry, pluck into bite-size pieces and place in a large bowl. For the dressing, mix the stock with vinegar and mustard. Stir in olive oil and season dressing with salt, and a pinch each of sugar and cayenne pepper.

7 Mix green salad with the dressing and arrange on a plate next to the Topfenpflanzerl.

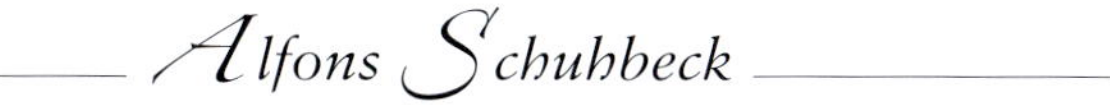

"According to taste, I add fried ceps (yellow boletuses), tarragon or bear's garlic to the Topfenflanzerl."

PICKLED MIESBACHER WITH CANDIED COCKTAIL TOMATOES

For the tomatoes:

5 oz (150 g) cocktail tomatoes
salt · 2 tsp icing sugar
1 garlic clove
1 tsp rosemary needles
4 tbsp mild olive oil

For the Miesbacher:

4 cubes Miesbacher cheese (a specialty of the Bavarian region Miesbach), each about 3 oz (80 g) or as an alternative: Romadur or Limburger

For the marinade:

2 shallots
1 2/3 cups (400 ml) vegetable stock
2–3 tbsp balsamic vinegar
1/3 cup (80 ml) olive oil
2 rosemary sprigs
2 small medium hot chili peppers
2 strips organic lemon peel
8 basil leaves
freshly ground pepper

4 servings

1 For the Tomatoes: Heat the oven to 210 °F (100 °C). Wash the cocktail tomatoes and cut in half. Place on cookie sheet with the cut side up and sprinkle with salt and icing sugar. Peel garlic, cut into slices and place between tomatoes. Chop rosemary needles and mix with the olive oil. Put drops of rosemary oil on the tomatoes and candy them on the middle rack for 1 1/2 to 2 hours.

2 For the Miesbacher: Cut each cheese cube into three slices and place in a suitable large flat dish or fill into a jar.

3 For the marinade: Peel the shallots and cut into thin rings. Stir the stock with vinegar and olive oil and pour over the cheese pieces. Place candied tomatoes, rosemary sprigs, chili peppers, lemon peel, basil leaves and shallot rings around the cheese and marinate together for at least 30 minutes. Remove the pickled Miesbacher from the marinade just before serving and grind coarse pepper on top.

"Candied cocktail tomatoes are the tastiest if they are cut in half and candied in the oven. It is particularly attractive if you leave a few tomatoes whole and candy them to use for garnishing."

Red Cabbage Salad

For the red cabbage:

1.3 lb (600 g) red cabbage
2 tbsp juice from preserved cranberries
3.4 fl oz (100 ml) freshly pressed orange juice

For the dressing:

5 tbsp red wine vinegar
salt · freshly ground pepper
1 tsp sugar · 4 tbsp oil

4 servings

1 For the cabbage: Clean red cabbage, remove outer leaves and core the stalk. Cut cabbage into fine strips or slices, place in a bowl and mix with cranberry juice and orange juice.

2 For the dressing: Mix vinegar with salt, pepper, sugar and oil. Mix the cabbage thoroughly with the dressing. Allow to infuse for at least 10 minutes and season the red cabbage once more with salt and pepper.

Bavarian Coleslaw

1.1 lb (500 g) young white (green) cabbage
salt
1 tbsp icing sugar
5 tbsp red wine vinegar
1/2 cup (125 ml) vegetable stock
3 tbsp oil
freshly ground pepper
caraway seeds
cayenne pepper · sugar
2 oz (50 g) streaky bacon

4 servings

1 Clean green cabbage, remove outer leaves and core the stalk. Slice the cabbage into fine strips and place in a metal bowl. Season lightly with salt.

2 Caramelize icing sugar in a pan over medium heat. Deglaze with vinegar and reduce to half the amount. Pour in the stock, boil once more, pour the hot cooking water over the cabbage and mix. Stir in two tablespoons oil and season with salt and pepper as well as a pinch of caraway seeds, cayenne pepper and some sugar. Allow to infuse for 10 minutes.

3 Cut the bacon into small cubes. Heat the remaining oil in a skillet and fry the bacon cubes over low heat until crisp. Remove the bacon cubes from skillet and drain on paper towel. Sprinkle bacon cubes over the cabbage salad and serve.

Home Fries Salad with Bratwurst

For the dressing:

1/2 cup (125 ml) vegetable stock
5 tbsp red wine vinegar
1 tbsp hot mustard · 2 slices garlic
salt · sugar · cayenne pepper
8 tbsp mild olive oil

For the salad:

1.7 lb (800 g) small low starch potatoes
salt · 1 tsp caraway seeds
1 bunch of arugula
2 bunches green onions
7 oz (200 g) wide green beans
1.5 lb (700 g) Nuremberger bratwurst
4 tbsp oil · freshly ground pepper
marjoram · ground caraway seeds

4 servings

1 For the dressing: Pour the stock with vinegar, mustard and garlic into a tall bowl and blend with a wand mixer. Season with salt, sugar, cayenne pepper and mix in the olive oil.

2 For the salad: Wash potatoes. Cook in abundant salted water with caraway seeds for about 15 minutes until soft. Strain, peel while still hot and cool off. Cut potatoes into slices.

3 Pick through arugula, wash and spin-dry. Clean green onions, wash and cut diagonally into 0.1 to 0.2 inch (3 to 5 cm) thick rings. Clean beans, wash and cut in half diagonally. Blanch in salted water for 5 minutes. Pour into a sieve, rinse off with cold water and drain. Cut bratwursts diagonally in thirds.

4 Heat one or two tablespoons oil in a skillet and fry the potatoes over medium heat. Add green onions and fry together for several minutes. Add beans. Season with salt and pepper as well as a pinch of marjoram and caraway seeds. Transfer the potato-bean mixture to a bowl.

5 Heat the remaining oil in a skillet and fry the sausages over medium heat. Drain on paper towel and let cool off. Add the bratwurst to the potato-bean mixture. Add arugula and dressing and mix everything carefully.

Cooking Bavarian White Sausages

salt
8 Bavarian white sausages (in German called Weisswurst)
2–3 strips organic lemon peel
2–3 parsley sprigs
sweet mustard

4 servings

1 Pour enough water into a large saucepan so that the sausages are well covered. Heat the water to 165 up to 175 °F (75 to 80 °C) and salt.

2 Place sausages into water. Add lemon peel and parsley sprigs.

3 Let the sausages sit for about 15 minutes. Do not boil otherwise they will burst. The sausages rise to the top when they are ready.

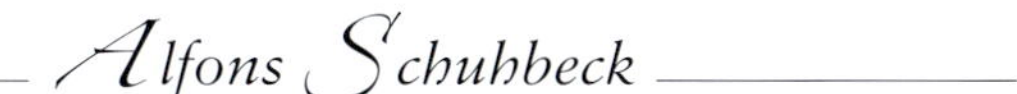

"Sweet mustard, which is also called Weisswurst mustard, is made out of coarsely ground mustard seeds sweetened with sugar and apple sauce."

POTATO SALAD WITH RADISHES

For the salad:

2.2 lb (1 kg) low starch potatoes
salt
1/2 tbsp caraway seeds
1 small onion · 2 tbsp oil
10–12 radishes
1/2 cucumber
2 tbsp brown butter (see below)
1 tbsp finely chopped chives

For the dressing:

1 2/3 cups (400 ml) poultry stock
3 tbsp red wine vinegar
1 tbsp hot mustard
salt · cayenne pepper · sugar

4 servings

1 Wash potatoes and cook in abundant salted water with caraway seeds until soft. Drain, peel while still hot and cool off. Cut the cooled-off potatoes into 0.1 to 0.2 inch (4 to 5 mm) thick slices and place in a bowl.

2 For the dressing: Heat the stock and stir in vinegar and mustard. Season with salt and a pinch each of cayenne pepper and sugar. Add a hand full of potato slices and mash with a wand mixer. Mix the dressing little by little into the potato slices so that they are able to adsorb the liquid.

3 Peel onion and dice finely. Heat a tablespoon oil in a skillet and braise onion cubes over low heat until translucent. Clean radishes, wash and cut into slices. Peel cucumbers and cut into slices. Fold brown butter, onion cubes, chives, radishes and cucumber slices into the potato salad. Grind coarse pepper on top to taste. The potato salad also tastes good by itself, without cucumbers and radishes. Otherwise, add only one – cucumbers or radishes – and substitute chives with parsley.

Alfons Schubbeck

"Depending on the season, I vary my potato salad by adding fried chanterelle, bear's garlic or other herbs. Pesto, pickled pumpkin or strips of endive are also suitable."

BROWN BUTTER

9 oz (250 g) butter

For about 1 cup (250 g)

1 Melt the butter in a small saucepan over medium heat and heat up slowly until it is golden brown and has a nutty aroma.

2 Remove from stove and pour the butter through a sieve that is covered with paper towel. Fill the brown butter into a tightly covered jar and keep in the refrigerator for later use.

Jellied Cured Meat from Bavarian Cockerel with Roasted Potatoes

To cure:

3.5 oz (100 g) each of salt and curing salt
2 bay leaves · 10 juniper berries
4 cloves
2 tsp mustard corns
1 thyme sprig
6–7 cockerel legs à 9 oz (250 g), with skin, ready to cook

For the jelly:

2 onions
4 oz (120 g) celeriac
2 carrots
2 yellow carrots (or carrots)
2 ribs celery · 1 bay leaf
3 juniper berries
1 tsp black peppercorns
3 slices ginger
10 leaves white gelatin
1 garlic clove, peeled and halved
1 strip organic lemon peel
1 thyme sprig
1 small dried chili pepper
5 tbsp Champagne vinegar or white balsamic vinegar
salt · sugar
oil for terrine

For the potatoes:

1.1 lb (500 g) small low starch potatoes, precooked, peeled and cut into slices
1–2 tbsp oil · salt
freshly ground pepper
dried marjoram
1 tsp caraway seeds

4 servings

1 To cure the chicken legs, start 6 days before the preparation of the jelly. In a large saucepan, boil about 2 quarts (2 liters) of water with the two types of salt. Remove from stove, add spices to the hot cure, and cool off. Rinse the chicken legs and place in cure liquid. Cover and refrigerate for 5 days.

2 For the Jelly: One day in advance, remove the chicken legs from cure liquid, drain and remove the liquid brine. Peel and quarter onions. Clean and peel carrots and celeriac. Slice celeriac into 0.4 inch (1 cm) thick spears. Cut carrots in half lengthwise. Wash and clean celery and cut in half.

3 In a large saucepan, bring about 3 quarts (3 liters) water to a boil. Add the cured chicken legs together with onion quarters and bring to a boil once more, skim foam off the surface. Gently simmer the chicken meat just below the boiling point for about 1 hour until tender. Add spices after 30 minutes. Add the remaining vegetables and cook until tender.

4 Remove the chicken legs from brew and take off skin. Release the meat from the bones and divide into single muscle groups. Pour the brew into a sieve, reserve celeriac, carrots and celery, remove onions. Degrease the chicken broth.

5 Soak the gelatin in cold water. Measure 2 1/2 cups (600 ml) of chicken broth and heat up in a saucepan. Add garlic, lemon peel, thyme sprig and chili pepper, let infuse 5 minutes in broth and remove. Remove saucepan from stove. Squeeze the gelatin well and dissolve while stirring in the hot broth. Season the broth generously with vinegar, salt and sugar.

6 Brush a terrine or a loaf pan (volume about 1.5 quarts / 1.5 liters) with oil and line with plastic wrap. Place the cured chicken meat and vegetables in alternating layers inside. Pour the lukewarm gelatin broth on top to just cover the layers. Reserve the remaining gelatin broth. Cover the jelly and let it become firm in refrigerator for at least 4 hours (ideally overnight).

7 With the aid of the plastic wrap, overturn the cured meat jelly and remove the wrap. Cut the cured meat jelly into slices using an electric knife and place on a plate. Warm up the remaining gelatin broth over low heat and brush over the jelly slices.

8 Roast the potato slices in a skillet with oil until golden brown. Season with salt and pepper and a pinch each of marjoram and caraway seeds. Arrange the roasted potatoes with the cured meat jelly on plates and serve with a salad of choice.

Sweet-sour Marinated Fried Trout

For the stock:

2 onions
1 tsp each of mustard corns, juniper berries, coriander corns and black peppercorns
1 tbsp oil · 1 tbsp sugar
5/8 cup (150 ml) wine vinegar
2 1/8 cups (500 ml) vegetable stock
1 garlic clove · 1 bay leaf
2 small dried chili peppers
1 tbsp each of dill tips and parsley leaves, freshly chopped
2 slices ginger

For the fish:

4 trout fillets à 3 oz (80 g), with skin, ready to cook
4 tbsp all purpose flour (ideally Wiener Griessler)
1–2 tbsp oil

4 servings

1 For the stock: Peel onions, cut in half and then into fine strips. Toast mustard corns, juniper berries, coriander and peppercorns in a saucepan without fat over low heat for about 1 minute until fragrant.

2 Add the oil to the spices in the saucepan and heat up. Add onion strips and braise over low heat until translucent. Stir in the sugar and deglaze with vinegar. Add vegetable stock. Peel garlic and cut in half. Add to stock together with bay leaf, chili peppers, dill, parsley and ginger. Bring the stock to a boil once, remove from stove, and pour into a flat oven-safe dish.

3 For the fish: Rinse the trout fillets, pat dry and cut crosswise in half. Put flour on a plate. Briefly coat the skin side of the fish fillets with flour. Heat the remaining oil in a skillet and sear the fillets with skin side down over medium heat for about 2 minutes until crisp.

4 Remove the fillets from skillet and place with the skin side up into the hot onion broth. Leave to cool off. Allow trout fillets to marinate covered in the refrigerator for several hours.

Alfons Schubbeck

"Fried trout can be prepared in advance and is ideal for buffets. Instead of trout, you can use vendace or arctic char."

Herb Vinaigrette

1 shallot
1/2 cup (125 ml) vegetable stock
2 tbsp red wine vinegar
1/2 tsp hot mustard
3 tbsp mild olive oil
3 sprigs each of parsley, chervil and basil
salt · freshly ground pepper
sugar

For about 7 fl oz (200 ml)

1 Peel shallot and dice very finely. Blend vegetable stock with vinegar and mustard. Add oil, first drop by drop, then in a thin stream while stirring vigorously with a whisk. Stir in the diced shallot.

2 Wash parsley, chervil and basil and shake dry. Pluck leaves off stems, chop finely, and mix into the vinaigrette. Season the herb vinaigrette with salt, pepper and a pinch of sugar. It goes well with all leafy salads.

Potato Yogurt Dressing

1 medium hot red chili pepper
1/2 potato, about 2 oz (60 g)
1 2/3 cups (400 ml) vegetable stock
1/2 small bay leaf
1/2 small garlic clove, peeled
1 tbsp lemon juice
3 tbsp olive oil
1.7 fl oz (50 g) plain yogurt
salt · freshly grated nutmeg
ground caraway seeds

For about 2 1/8 cups or 1 pint (500 ml)

1 Cut the chili pepper lengthwise in half. Remove the seeds and rinse the pulp. Peel potato, wash, and cut into 0.2 inch (5 mm) cubes. Bring the stock to a boil in a saucepan and add bay leaf. Gently simmer chili pepper and potato in the stock just below the boiling point for 10 to 15 minutes until tender. Remove bay leaf.

2 Fill potato cubes together with stock and chili pepper into a tall container. Add garlic, lemon juice, olive oil and yogurt, and purée with a wand mixer until smooth. Season with salt, some nutmeg and a small pinch of caraway. This dressing goes well with crisp salad, particularly lamb's lettuce.

Mustard Dressing

3.4 fl oz (100 ml) vegetable stock
1 tsp sweet mustard
1 tsp hot mustard
1 tsp sour cream
1 tbsp balsamic vinegar
1 tbsp red wine vinegar
5 tbsp mild olive oil · salt
freshly ground pepper
a pinch of cayenne pepper

For about 7 fl oz (200 ml)

For the dressing, blend the stock with sweet and hot mustard, sour cream and both types of vinegar in a small bowl with a whisk. Stir in the olive oil little by little. Season the dressing with salt, pepper and cayenne pepper. It goes well with crisp greens and colorful vegetable salads.

Asparagus with Marinated Arctic Char and Egg Marinade

For the Arctic char:

2 tsp coriander corns
1 tsp black peppercorns
1 tbsp juniper berries
1 tsp each of fennel seeds and mustard corns
4 arctic char fillets à 3 oz (80 g), with skin, ready to cook
1.8 oz (50 g) salt · 3 tbsp sugar
1 tbsp parsley leaves and dill tips, freshly chopped
1 tbsp each of grated organic lemon and orange zest

For the asparagus:

8 stalks white asparagus
1–2 tbsp salt · 1 tbsp sugar

For the marinade:

2 eggs, hard-boiled
1/3 cup (80 ml) vegetable stock
1/2 tsp hot mustard
1–2 tbsp red wine vinegar
3–4 tbsp mild olive oil
salt · freshly ground pepper
sugar

Additional ingredients:

1 tbsp finely chopped chives

4 servings

1 For marinating the char, a day in advance, toast coriander corns, peppercorns, juniper berries, fennel seeds and mustard corns in a non-stick skillet without fat until fragrant. Finely grind the spice mixture with mortar and pestle or a turbo blender.

2 Rinse the char fillets and pat dry. In a small bowl, mix salt, sugar, the spice mixture, parsley, dill, lemon and orange zest. Spread the mixture over both sides of the char fillets, wrap the fillets in plastic wrap and leave to infuse in the refrigerator overnight.

3 For the asparagus: The next day, peel the asparagus stalks and cut off woody ends. In a large saucepan, bring about 2 quarts (2 liters) water to a boil and add salt and sugar. Add asparagus and boil for 8 to 10 minutes, depending on thickness.

4 Remove the asparagus, refresh with cold water and drain. Cover and set aside at room temperature until ready to use.

5 For the marinade: Peel eggs and cut in half. Separate egg yolks and egg whites and chop finely separately.

6 In a small bowl, use a whisk to blend the stock with mustard, vinegar and olive oil. Generously season the marinade with salt, pepper and a pinch of sugar. Finish by stirring in the chopped eggs.

7 To serve, place two asparagus stalks on each plate, drizzle with the egg marinade and sprinkle with finely chopped chives. Take the marinated char from the refrigerator, scrape of the marinade with the back of a knife removing the skin at the same time. Cut the char into slices, arrange with the asparagus, and garnish to taste with small, marinated lettuce leaves and blossoms.

"Arctic char can be substituted with marinated trout fillets (see page 30), marinated salmon slices or raw tuna fish slices. Marinate the tuna slices with a few drops of lemon juice, some olive oil, salt and freshly ground pepper. Half of the asparagus can be substituted with green asparagus."

Beef Tartare with Rösti and Cauliflower Remoulade

For the beef tartare:

1.1 lb (500 g) fillet of beef or fillet tips
1 small pickle·1–2 tsp capers
3 pickled anchovy fillets
1/2 onion · 1 tbsp oil
2 tbsp mild olive oil
1 tbsp tomato ketchup
1 tbsp sweet-sour chili sauce
2 tbsp finely chopped chives
a dash of lemon juice
1 pinch of sweet paprika powder
salt · freshly ground pepper
sugar

For the remoulade:

5 oz (150 g) cauliflower flowerets
7 oz (200 g) crème fraîche or as an alternative: sour cream
2 tbsp milk · 1/2 tsp hot mustard
2 pickled anchovy fillets
1 tsp capers
1 pinch of grated organic lemon or lime zest
1–2 tbsp finely chopped chives
1 tbsp red wine vinegar
a few drops of Worcestershire sauce
salt · freshly ground pepper
cayenne pepper

For the Rösti (hash brown potatoes):

2 low starch potatoes, about 9 oz (250 g)
salt · freshly ground pepper
freshly grated nutmeg
3 tbsp oil

4 servings

1 For the beef tartare: Remove fat and tendons from the meat and mince in a meat grinder. Finely chop pickle, capers and anchovy fillets. Peel and finely dice onion. Heat the oil in a skillet and braise the onion cubes over low heat until translucent and cool off.

2 In a bowl, mix well minced beef with diced onion, pickle, capers, anchovy, olive oil, ketchup, chili sauce and chives. Season the minced beef generously with lemon juice, paprika powder, salt, pepper and a pinch of sugar.

3 For the remoulade: Wash the cauliflower flowerets, separate into very small flowerets and cook in salted water for 6 to 7 minutes until almost soft. Pour into a sieve, refresh with cold water and drain.

4 Stir the crème fraîche with milk and mustard in a small bowl until smooth. Finely chop anchovies and capers and add together with lemon zest and chives to the mustard cream. Stir to mix. Mix in the cauliflower flowerets. Season the remoulade with vinegar, Worcestershire sauce, salt, pepper and a pinch of cayenne pepper.

5 For the Rösti: Wash and peel potatoes and shred with a vegetable grater into fine strips. Season with salt, pepper and nutmeg. Allow the potatoes to infuse for 1 to 2 minutes and press out the juice with hands.

6 Heat the oil in a large non-stick skillet, divide the potato strips into four portions and place like flat cakes into the pan. Roast Rösti in hot oil portionwise over low heat until golden brown. Turn over and fry on the other side until brown as well. Remove from skillet and drain on paper towel.

7 Divide the beef tartare into four tartare steaks and arrange on plates with Rösti and cauliflower remoulade.

Baked Bavarian White Sausage Wheels on Lentil Salad

For the salad:

7 oz (200 g) small green lentils (puy lentils)
1 onion
2 oz (50 g) streaky bacon
1 tbsp oil · 1 tsp tomato paste
1 bay leaf
1 2/3 cups (400 ml) poultry stock
2 oz (50 g) each of carrots, celeriac, leeks
dried marjoram
4 tbsp balsamic vinegar
1 tbsp very mild olive oil
2 tbsp brown butter (see page 26)
salt · freshly ground pepper
sugar · cayenne pepper
1 slice ginger ·1 slice garlic
1 strip organic orange peel
1 small sliver of cinnamon bark (to taste)

For the white sausage wheels:

6 Bavarian white sausages (Weisswurst)
2 eggs·salt
freshly ground pepper
a dash of lemon juice
3.5 oz (100 g) all purpose flour (ideally Wiener Griessler)
3.5 oz (100 g) white bread crumbs
oil for frying

4 servings

1 For the salad: Soak lentils for 2 hours in cold water. Peel and finely dice onion. Cut bacon into small cubes. Heat oil in a saucepan and lightly braise the onion and bacon cubes. Drain lentils and add to saucepan. Stir in the tomato paste and braise some more. Add bay leaf and pour in the stock. Simmer lentils for 20 minutes.

2 Clean the vegetables, peel or wash and dice finely. Add diced carrot and celeriac after 10 minutes cooking time to lentils and stir. Season with a pinch of marjoram. Add diced leek a few minutes before the end of cooking time. Remove saucepan from stove and let the lentils cool off a bit.

3 Season the lentil salad with balsamic vinegar, olive oil, brown butter, salt, pepper, and a pinch each of sugar and cayenne pepper. Add ginger, garlic, orange peel and if desired a small sliver of cinnamon bark. Let the whole spices infuse the salad for 5 to 10 minutes and remove again.

4 For the white sausage wheels: Remove the skin from the sausages and cut the sausages diagonally into 0.6 to 0.8 inch (1 1/2 to 2 cm) thick slices. Whisk eggs in a deep plate and season with salt, pepper and lemon juice. Prepare two deep plates, one with the flour and one with white bread crumbs. Coat the sausage slices first in flour, carefully dredge through the whisked eggs and finally coat with white bread crumbs.

5 Fill a skillet finger deep with oil and heat up. Fry the sausage wheels over medium heat on both sides until golden brown. Remove with a skimmer and drain on paper towel.

6 Arrange the lukewarm lentil salad on warmed plates, put the Bavarian white sausage wheels on top and serve immediately.

"It is important that the slices for the Bavarian white sausage wheels – in German called Weisswurstradel – are not too thin so they do not dry out when frying."

Soups & Stews

Beef Bouillon

2.6 lb (1.2 kg) beef brisket, ready to cook
1–2 tbsp oil
2 onions
1 carrot
5 oz (150 g) celeriac
3.5 oz (100 g) leek
1 bay leaf
3 juniper berries
1/2 tsp black peppercorns
1 strip organic lemon peel
5 parsley sprigs
1 small lovage leaf
2 slices garlic
1 slice ginger
salt
freshly grated nutmeg

4 servings

1 Brown the entire beef brisket in a pan with oil over medium heat. Place in a large saucepan and fill with about 3 quarts (3 liters) water so that the meat is covered. Cook the meat for 3 hours just below the boiling point over medium heat until it is tender. Skim off foam while cooking.

2 In the meantime, peel onions and add the onion peels to the saucepan with meat.

3 Peel carrot and celeriac and cut together with the onions into about 0.6 inch (1 1/2 cm) pieces. Clean leek, cut in half lengthwise, wash and cut into 0.6 inch (1 1/2 cm) long pieces. Add onion, carrot and celeriac pieces as well as bay leaf, juniper berries and peppercorns after 2 1/4 to 2 1/2 hours of cooking time to meat. Add leek 15 minutes before the end of cooking time.

4 Take out the meat, strain broth carefully through a sieve into a saucepan. Let lemon peel, parsley sprigs, lovage, garlic and ginger infuse the broth for several minutes, then remove again and season the soup with salt. To serve, grate nutmeg into warmed soup bowls and the pour soup on top. According to taste and preference, add carrot and celeriac pieces.

"The boiled beef can be sliced thin and marinated as beef salad. Beef brisket tastes also delicious if the cooked meat is cut into 0.2 inch (5 mm) thick slices. Spread a thin layer of hot mustard on both sides, and coat with all purpose flour. Fry meat golden brown in some oil over low heat. This beef brisket with mustard crust is excellent served on top of leafy salads."

Semolina Dumplings

2 oz (50 g) soft butter
1 egg (room temperature)
3 oz (80 g) semolina
salt
freshly grated nutmeg

4 servings

1 Cream butter until light and fluffy, add egg and whisk until blended well. Stir in semolina and season the mixture with salt and nutmeg. Allow the semolina mixture to soak for at least 1 hour at room temperature.

2 Bring a pot of salted water to the boiling point. Shape uniform size dumplings from the semolina mixture with two wet teaspoons, dipping spoons into hot water between the shaping of dumplings. Gently simmer semolina dumplings in salted water just below the boiling point for about 15 minutes until done. Remove with a skimmer. Serve the semolina dumplings, like saffron semolina dumplings (see recipe below).

"To have butter and egg blend well, separate egg and stir in first the egg yolk, then the egg white. To maintain the creaminess of butter it is important that the egg is not too cold. In Bavaria, the semolina dumplings are called Griessnockerl."

Saffron Semolina Dumplings

3/4 cup (175 ml) vegetable stock
1 small envelope saffron stigmas, 0.06 dram (0.1 g), finely ground
3/4 cup (175 ml) milk
4 oz (120 g) durum wheat semolina
salt · freshly ground pepper
freshly grated nutmeg
1/2 tsp grated organic orange zest
1 egg yolk ·1 egg
1 bay leaf

For about 16 dumplings

1 For the semolina dumplings, heat the vegetable stock in a pot, remove from stove, and sprinkle in saffron. Allow to infuse for 10 minutes. Add milk and bring to a boil. Let semolina trickle in and boil to reduce over low heat for several minutes while stirring until thick.

2 Season the semolina mixture with salt, pepper, nutmeg and orange zest, remove from stove and cool off. Beat egg yolk with egg and stir into semolina mixture. In a large saucepan, bring to a boil a large quantity of salted water with the bay leaf. Shape semolina dumplings using two wet soupspoons and gently simmer just below the boiling point for 10 minutes until done.

3 For serving a soup, grate nutmeg into a hot bowl, according to taste. Add small pieces of vegetables, poultry pieces, slices of cooked sausage meat and the saffron semolina dumplings. Fill up the soup bowl with hot stock, round off with sherry, and sprinkle finely chopped chives on top.

Chicken Soup

1 onion
3.3 lb (1.5 kg) chicken legs
2 ribs of celery
1 carrot
1 parsley root
1 long thin leek
1–2 tbsp dried button mushrooms, as an alternative: 2 oz (50 g) fresh button mushrooms
1 bay leaf
1 tsp black peppercorns
4 allspice corns
1 slice ginger
salt
freshly grated nutmeg
1 tbsp medium sherry

4 servings

1 For the soup, peel the onion and set both onion and peels aside. Rinse the chicken legs and pat dry.

2 In a large pot, bring about 2.5 quarts (2.5 liters) water to a boil. Add chicken legs and onion peels and gently simmer just below the boiling point for just over 1 hour. Skim foam off regularly with a skimmer.

3 In the meantime, clean celery, wash, and cut into quarters. Peel carrots and parsley roots and cut lengthwise. Cut the onion that has been set aside into quarters. Clean leek, cut lengthwise and wash. Add prepared vegetables, button mushrooms, bay leaf as well as peppercorns, allspice corns and ginger to the chicken brew after 30 minutes cooking time.

4 Remove chicken legs and skin. Take off meat from bones and cut into smaller pieces. Pour soup through a fine strainer that has been lined with a cheese cloth or paper towel. Salt the soup. Remove carrot, parsley root and celery pieces from strainer and cut into smaller pieces. Take out button mushrooms, onions, leek and spices.

5 To serve, grate a bit of nutmeg into a warmed soup bowl and add cut-up vegetables, chicken and saffron semolina dumplings (see page 39). According to taste, sprinkle finely chopped chives on top.

"If I intend to add the leek to soups, I only add it 10 minutes before the end of cooking time."

Pancake Strips

2 eggs
2.5 oz (70 g) flour
3/4 cup (170 ml) milk
3–4 tbsp melted butter (lukewarm)
1 tbsp freshly chopped parsley leaves
salt
freshly ground pepper
freshly grated nutmeg
butter for frying

4 servings

1 Beat the eggs in a bowl. Add flour and stir well. Pour in milk a little bit at a time while stirring and continue stirring all ingredients until batter is smooth. Fold in melted butter and parsley. Season the pancake batter with salt, pepper and a pinch of nutmeg. Cover the batter and allow to rest for about 30 minutes.

2 Melt some butter in a skillet over low heat. Pour the batter into the skillet with a small ladle. Tilt and rotate the skillet to spread the batter evenly and make a thin coating. Turn over the pancake as soon as the bottom is golden brown. Brown the other side as well and remove from skillet. Repeat the process for the remaining pancakes and stack the finished pancakes one on top of another so they do not dry out. To serve, cut them into strips that are not larger than 0.2 inch (5 mm) wide and add to the hot stock.

Ham Schöberl

2 oz (50 g) flour
1 knife tip baking powder
3.5 oz (100 g) cooked ham
2 oz (50 g) soft butter
4 egg yolks (room temperature)
freshly ground pepper
freshly grated nutmeg
4 egg whites
salt
5 tbsp cream

4 servings

1 Heat the oven to 350 °F (180 °C). Mix flour with baking powder and sift. Cut ham into small cubes.

2 Cream butter until fluffy, fold in egg yolks one after another and whisk the mixture until light and foamy. Season the mixture with pepper and a pinch of nutmeg. Beat the egg white with a pinch of salt until it forms soft peaks. Fold the beaten egg white and the sifted flour into the butter mixture. Gradually stir in the cream.

3 Line a casserole dish in the size of about 8 to 12 inches (20 x 30 cm) with parchment paper. Spread the Schöberl batter in a 0.2 to 0.4 inch (5 to 10 mm) thick layer on parchment paper and sprinkle with ham cubes.

4 Bake in the oven on the middle rack for about 15 minutes until golden brown. Cool off and cut into 0.8 inch (2 cm) large diamond shapes.

Alfons Schuhbeck

"The Ham Schöberl – in German called Schinkenschöberl – freeze really well. They can be stored in the freezer in an airtight freezer container or freezer bag. Add the Schöberl still frozen directly to hot stock."

Liver Dumplings

1/2 onion
1 tbsp oil
9 oz (250 g) white bread, without crust
1 egg · 1 egg yolk
1 tsp hot mustard
1/2 cup (125 ml) milk
10 oz (300 g) veal liver, cleaned and put through meat grinder or cut into small pieces with a food processor
dried marjoram
salt
freshly ground pepper
freshly grated nutmeg
a pinch of grated organic lemon zest
1 tbsp freshly chopped parsley leaves
1 bay leaf
1 strip organic lemon peel

4 servings

1 Peel onion and cut into fine dice. Heat the oil in a pan and braise the onion dice over low heat until translucent. Cut white bread into 0.2 to 0.4 inch (5 to 10 mm) cubes.

2 Stir egg with egg yolk and mustard. Heat milk, and combine with the egg mixture. Pour over white bread and mix lightly. Add veal liver, onion dice, a pinch each of marjoram, salt, pepper, nutmeg, lemon zest and parsley, and mix well. Form eight dumplings from the mixture with wet hands.

3 Heat a pot of salted water to the boiling point and add bay leaf and lemon peel. Let the dumplings gently simmer in salted water below the boiling point for 8 minutes until done. Remove dumplings with a skimmer and allow to drain on paper towel. Serve the dumplings in a clear soup.

"Veal liver can be substituted with any other livers such as poultry, turkey or beef liver. To make baked liver dumplings, deep fry formed dumplings at 325 °F (160 °C) until brown. Finally let dumplings simmer in hot soup for another 5 minutes. If desired, shape dumplings smaller and coat with white bread crumbs before frying."

Green Krapferl

For the Krapferl (ravioli) dough:

5 oz (150 g) all purpose flour (ideally Wiener Griessler)
1 egg · 1 egg yolk
2 tbsp mild olive oil
salt

For the stuffing:

1/4 onion
1 tsp oil
10 oz (300 g) spinach
salt
2 oz (50 g) herbal leaves, e.g. parsley, bear's garlic, watercress, dill, tarragon, chervil
1/2 cup (120 g) cream cheese (double cream)
1 egg yolk
a pinch of grated organic lemon zest
freshly ground pepper

Additional ingredients:

flour to roll out dough
1 egg white
semolina for cookie sheet
salt

For about 20 Krapferl

1 For the Krapferl dough: Combine flour with egg, egg yolk, olive oil and a pinch of salt, and knead by hand or with a food processor until dough is smooth and elastic. Wrap the dough in plastic wrap and refrigerate for at least 30 minutes.

2 For the stuffing: Peel and finely dice onion. Heat the oil in a pan, braise the onion cubes over low heat until translucent. Pick through the spinach, wash, drain, and remove coarse stems. Blanch the spinach in boiling salted water for about 3 minutes. Pour into a sieve, rinse off with cold water and drain. Press out water well with hands and chop the spinach into fine pieces. Wash herbs, shake dry and cut into small pieces. Mix well onion, spinach, herbs, cream cheese, egg yolk and lemon zest. Season with salt, pepper and nutmeg.

3 To complete, cut the dough into quarters and roll out with a pasta machine or rolling pin to four long, thin sheets of dough. Beat the egg white and thinly brush two long pieces of dough. Place the stuffing on the sheets of dough with a teaspoon 0.8 to 1.2 inches (2 to 3 cm) apart and cover with the two remaining sheets of dough lightly and as smoothly as possible. Press the upper dough layer with fingers around the stuffing. Cut out ravioli with a round cutter (about 1.6 inches / 4 cm diameter) and seal edges tightly. Set ravioli aside on a cookie sheet that has been dusted with semolina until ready to use.

4 Cook the ravioli in salted water just below the boiling point for 3 to 4 minutes until firm to the bite. Remove ravioli with a skimmer and allow to drain. Serve the Krapferl in clear soup.

Alfons Schuhbeck

"The green Krapferl – a special Bavarian sort of ravioli stuffed with spinach and herbs – can be added to clear meat, vegetable or fish soups as well as cream soups. Another option is to turn them in brown butter (see page 26) and brown onions and serve them with leafy salad as a dish by itself."

Swabian Pockets Stuffed with Potatoes and Bacon

For the dough:

5 oz (150 g) all purpose flour (ideally Wiener Griessler)
1 egg · 1 egg yolk
2 tbsp mild olive oil
salt

For the stuffing:

10 oz (300 g) high starch potatoes
salt
caraway seeds
3.5 oz (100 g) streaky bacon
$\frac{1}{2}$ onion
1 $\frac{1}{2}$ tbsp oil
$\frac{1}{4}$ cup (60 ml) hot milk
1 tbsp sour cream
2 tbsp brown butter (see page 26)
freshly ground pepper
caraway seeds
dried marjoram
freshly grated nutmeg

Additional ingredients:

flour to roll out dough
1 egg white
semolina for cookie sheet
salt

4 servings

1 For the dough: Combine flour, egg, egg yolk, olive oil and a pinch of salt. Knead with hands or with a food processor until dough is smooth and elastic. Wrap the dough in plastic wrap and refrigerate at least 30 minutes.

2 For the stuffing: Wash potatoes and boil in salted water with a pinch of caraway seeds until tender. Peel while they are still hot and mash with a potato masher. Cut bacon into small cubes. Peel and finely dice onion. Heat a tablespoon oil in a pan and brown the bacon cubes over medium heat until crispy and allow to drain on paper towel. Braise the onion cubes in the remaining oil over low heat until translucent. Stir the potatoes into hot milk, and fold in bacon, onion cubes, sour cream and brown butter. Season with salt, pepper and a pinch each of caraway seeds, marjoram and nutmeg. Fill the mixture into a piping bag with a nozzle of 0.3 to 0.4 inch (8 to 10 mm) in diameter.

3 To complete, cut dough in half and roll out with a pasta machine or a rolling pin into two thin sheets, about 4.7 inches (12 cm) wide while dusting with some flour. Beat the egg white. Cut each sheet of dough lengthwise in half and coat both pieces with the beaten egg white. Squeeze the stuffing along the middle of each long sheet of dough. Roll up lengthwise to obtain four long thin rolls with the dough seams on the bottom. Using the handle of a wooden spoon, press down on rolls at 1 to 1.2 inch (2 $\frac{1}{2}$ to 3 cm) intervals so that almost 0.4 inch (1 cm) of the dough is pressed together in between segments. Cut through the middle of the pressed down dough sections and seal the Swabian pockets with fingers. Set aside on a cookie sheet dusted with semolina until ready to use.

4 Let the Swabian pockets gently simmer in salted water just below the boiling point for 3 to 4 minutes. Remove with a skimmer and serve in a clear soup.

"Browned onion cubes give Swabian pockets – in Bavarian called Maultascherl – a hearty flavor: Finely dice an onion and brown lightly in a tablespoon butter with a pinch of sugar. Add to the bacon and mix into the stuffing. If I have planned to serve the Swabian pockets as a separate dish, I sprinkle some extra browned onion dice or onion rings on top."

Carrot Soup with Ginger

For the soup:

9 oz (250 g) carrots
1 large onion
1 tomato
2 tsp icing sugar
3 1/3 cups (800 ml) vegetable stock
1 red apple
1 tsp finely chopped ginger
2 slices garlic
1/2–1 tsp mild curry powder
7 fl oz (200 g) cream
4 tbsp cold butter

For the spice grinder:

1 tsp each of coriander corns, allspice corns, black peppercorns
1/2 tsp crushed cinnamon bark

4 servings

1 Peel carrots and onion und cut into small pieces. Wash tomatoes, remove core (not the seeds) and cut into small pieces.

2 Caramelize one teaspoon of icing sugar in a saucepan over low heat. Add vegetables and braise lightly. Pour in vegetable stock and cook vegetables just below the boiling point for 20 minutes.

3 Wash apples, core and cut into quarters. Cut the quarters into thin wedges. Peel two apple wedges, cut into small pieces and add to soup together with ginger, garlic and curry powder. Fill a spice grinder with coriander corns, allspice corns, peppercorns and cinnamon bark and season the soup with the spice blend. Add cream and three tablespoons of butter and purée soup with a wand mixer until smooth.

4 Caramelize the remaining icing sugar in a skillet over medium heat. Add the unpeeled apple wedges and the remaining butter and lightly brown the wedges on both sides.

5 To serve, whisk the soup once more with a wand mixer until foamy, pour in warmed soup bowls and garnish with apple slices.

Alfons Schuhbeck

"The onion can be substituted with a half of a thin stalk of leek. For the rest, prepare the soup as described above."

liter
1
0,9
0,8
0,7
0,6
0,5
0,4
0,3
0,2

Herb Soup

3.5 oz (100 g) fresh baby spinach
salt
3.5 oz (100 g) herbal leaves, e.g. basil, chervil, parsley, dill, stinging nettle, bear's garlic and sorrel
1 onion
1 potato, about 2.5 oz (70 g)
1 oz (30 g) cold butter
4 1/8 cups (1 liter) poultry stock
7 fl oz (200 g) cream
1 strip organic lemon peel
1 garlic clove, peeled and cut into slices
cayenne pepper
freshly grated nutmeg

4 servings

1 Pick through the spinach leaves, wash, drain and remove coarse stems. Blanch in boiling salted water for 3 minutes. Pour into a sieve, rinse off with cold water and allow to drain. Squeeze out water with hands and mince. Wash the herb leaves, shake dry and chop into small pieces. Peel the onion and potato and cut into small cubes.

2 Melt a tablespoon of butter in a saucepan, braise onion and potato cubes over low heat until onions are translucent. Fill saucepan up with stock and simmer just below the boiling point for 25 minutes. Add cream and purée the soup with a wand mixer or a food processor. Add lemon peel, allow to infuse for few more minutes and remove again.

3 Add spinach, herbs, garlic and remaining butter to the soup just before serving and mix with wand mixer. Season with salt, a pinch cayenne pepper and some nutmeg. Serve the soup immediately in warmed soup bowls.

Sweet Chestnut Soup with Truffle

1.1 lb (500 g) sweet chestnuts
1 tsp icing sugar
3 1/3 cups (800 ml) poultry stock
7 fl oz (200 g) cream
3 tbsp butter
0.3 oz (10 g) fresh truffle or a few dashes of white truffle oil
salt
cayenne pepper

4 servings

1 Heat the oven to 400 °F (200 °C). Cut chestnut shells on the bulging side crosswise with a sharp knife. Place chestnuts on a cookie sheet and bake in the oven on the middle rack for 10 to 15 minutes until the shells open. Peel chestnuts while they are still warm, also remove the thin inner skin.

2 Sift icing sugar into a saucepan and caramelize over medium heat. Pour in stock and add chestnuts. Simmer the soup just below the boiling point for 20 minutes until the chestnuts are cooked.

3 Purée the soup finely with a wand mixer, add cream and warm up. Mix in butter and truffle or truffle oil with a wand mixer. Season the soup with salt and cayenne pepper. Before serving, whisk once more with the wand mixer and pour into warmed soup bowls.

Squash Soup with Curry

1.3 lb (600 g) 'Muscade de provence' pumpkin or as an alternative butternut squash e.g. Waltham Butternut
3 1/8 cups (750 ml) poultry stock
5/8 cup (150 g) cream
1 tbsp mild curry powder
1 garlic clove, halved · 1 slice ginger
1 sliver of cinnamon bark
1/2 scraped out vanilla pod
1.4 oz (40 g) cold butter · salt

4 servings

1 Peel squash, remove core and seeds with a spoon. Cut the squash into 0.4 inch (1 cm) cubes.

2 Place the squash cubes with the stock in a saucepan and simmer just below the boiling point for 20 minutes until cooked. Add cream and curry powder and purée finely with a wand mixer.

3 Add garlic, ginger, cinnamon bark and vanilla pod to soup, allow to infuse for several minutes and remove again. Fold in the cold butter and season the soup with salt and curry powder.

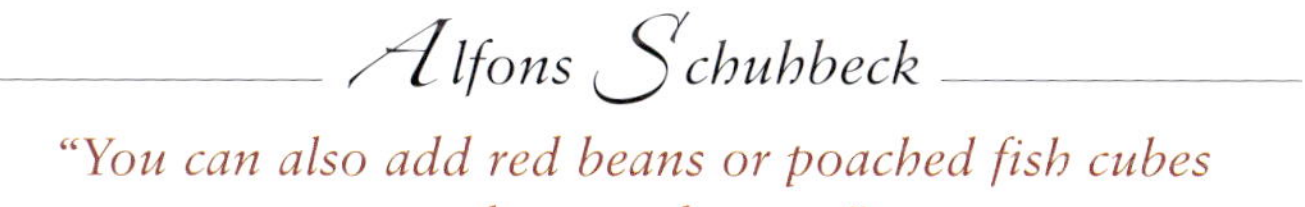

"You can also add red beans or poached fish cubes to the squash soup."

Potato Soup

1 onion
3 oz (80 g) celeriac
1 carrot
1.3 lb (600 g) potatoes
3 1/3 cups (800 ml) vegetable stock
1 bay leaf
1 small dried chili pepper
7 fl oz (200 g) cream
2 slices garlic
salt · dried marjoram
ground caraway seeds
1 strip organic lemon peel
freshly ground pepper
freshly grated nutmeg
1 tbsp freshly chopped parsley leaves

4 servings

1 Peel onion, celeriac, and carrot and cut into 0.2 to 0.4 inch (5 to 10 mm) cubes. Peel potatoes, wash and cut lengthwise into quarters. Cook potatoes in vegetable stock covered for about 40 minutes. After 20 minutes, add vegetable cubes as well as bay leaf and chili pepper. Remove potatoes from broth with a skimmer. Remove bay leaf and chili pepper. Mash potatoes and return to soup.

2 Pour the cream into the soup. Rub garlic with a bit of salt and add to the soup together with marjoram, caraway seeds and lemon peel. Simmer for 5 minutes over low heat and then remove lemon peel. Season the soup with salt, pepper and nutmeg.

3 Serve the soup in warmed soup bowls and sprinkle with parsley. The potato soup gets a heartier flavor if scallion rings are added with the spices. Additional ingredients like cooked ham cut into cubes or finely cut button mushrooms are also suitable.

Sweet-sour Marinated Rostbratwurst

1 large onion
1.1 lb (500 g) Nuremberger rostbratwurst
3 juniper berries
5 allspice corns
1 tsp black peppercorns
1 tbsp icing sugar
4 1/8 cups (1 liter) poultry stock
1 small bay leaf
4 tbsp red wine vinegar
salt · cayenne pepper
1 tbsp sugar
1 garlic clove
1 strip organic lemon peel
1 slice ginger
1.4 oz (40 g) cold butter
2 tbsp freshly chopped chives

4 servings

1 Peel the onion and cut into 0.2 inch (5 mm) cubes. Cut the sausages into 0.2 to 0.4 inch (5 to 10 mm) thick slices. Fill a small spice bag with juniper berries, allspice and peppercorns.

2 Dust icing sugar into a saucepan and caramelize over medium heat. Add the onion cubes and braise until translucent. Add stock, bay leaf and the small spice bag. Simmer the onions just below the boiling point for about 10 minutes.

3 Season the soup with vinegar, a bit of salt, and a pinch each of cayenne pepper and sugar. Peel garlic, cut in half and add together with sausage slices, lemon peel and ginger. Allow to infuse for 3 minutes. Remove the small spice bag and all the spices.

4 Pour the broth through a strainer into a saucepan and mix in the butter with a wand mixer. Season with sugar, salt and vinegar. Arrange the rostbratwursts and vegetables in warmed soup bowls, pour soup on top and serve sprinkled with chives.

"For a more colorful stew, add and cook with the onions: 1 carrot, 3.5 oz (100 g) celeriac and 1 to 2 potatoes cut into 0.4 to 0.8 inch (1 to 2 cm) cubes. Cooking time will increase by about 5 minutes. It is a good idea to use a spice bag, if many of the spices need to be removed from the dish at the end of cooking time. Good choices for a suitable spice bag are a tea egg or disposable tea bags closed with a clip."

Goulash Soup

For the soup:

1.5 lb (700 g) beef from the calf or shoulder
14 oz (400 g) onions
1–2 tbsp oil
1 tbsp tomato paste
3 1/8 cups (750 ml) poultry stock
1/2 each of yellow and red bell peppers
1/2 zucchini
14 oz (400 g) potatoes
salt · cayenne pepper
1 bay leaf

For the goulash seasoning:

2 garlic cloves
2 strips organic lemon peel
1/2 tsp caraway seeds
1/2 tsp dried marjoram
1/2–1 tbsp sweet paprika powder
1–2 tbsp poultry stock or water

Additional ingredients:

2 tbsp freshly chopped parsley leaves

4 servings

1 For the soup: Remove fat and large tendons from the beef and cut the beef into 0.4 inch (1 cm) cubes. Peel onions, cut in half and then into small cubes. Heat the oil in a large flat saucepan and brown the pieces of meat on all sides over medium heat and remove. Add the onion cubes to the pot and braise until translucent. Stir in the tomato paste and braise lightly for several minutes. Return the meat cubes to the pot and pour the poultry stock on top. Simmer covered for about 2 1/2 hours just below the boiling point over low heat.

2 In the meantime, core red and yellow bell peppers, wash and cut into 0.2 to 0.4 inch (5 to 10 mm) cubes. Wash zucchini and cut into cubes like bell peppers. Wash potatoes, peel and cut into 0.4 in (1 cm) cubes.

3 After 2 hours of cooking time, add bell peppers, zucchini and potato cubes to soup. Season with salt and a pinch cayenne pepper. Add bay leaf and cook for another 30 minutes.

4 For the goulash seasoning: Peel garlic, cut into slices and finely chop with lemon peel, caraway seeds and marjoram. Stir the paprika powder with a bit of cold stock or cold water until smooth. Season the goulash soup with some of the seasoning mix and the stirred paprika powder. Allow to infuse for 5 minutes.

5 Remove bay leaf from soup. Season the goulash soup with salt and pepper. Serve in warmed soup bowls and sprinkle parsley on top.

"It is better to season, check flavor and season again, rather than adding the entire quantity of goulash seasoning to the soup at once. Left over spice mixture can be mixed with some butter, wrapped in plastic wrap and stored for several days in the refrigerator or for several weeks in the freezer."

Mushrooms in Cream Sauce

1 small onion
2 tbsp oil
2 1/2 cups (600 ml) vegetable stock
1 small bay leaf
3 tbsp dried meadow mushrooms
5/8 cup (150 g) cream
1–2 tsp cornstarch
0.7 oz (20 g) cold butter
1 garlic clove
1 strip organic lemon peel
salt
freshly ground pepper
ground caraway seeds
cayenne pepper
1.3 lb (600 g) fresh mushrooms, e.g. ceps (boletuses), chanterelle or button mushrooms
1 tbsp freshly chopped parsley leaves

4 servings

1 Peel and finely dice onion. Heat a tablespoon oil in a saucepan and braise the onion cubes until translucent. Pour in the stock, add bay leaf and cook the onion about 10 minutes until done. Add meadow mushrooms and remove from stove. Allow to infuse for 20 minutes.

2 Remove bay leaf. Add cream, whisk the soup with a wand mixer and strain through a sieve into a saucepan.

3 Bring the soup to a boil again. Dissolve the cornstarch in a little bit of cold water and stir until smooth. Add to soup and gently boil for another 2 minutes. Stir in the butter. Peel garlic, cut in half and add to the soup together with lemon peel. Simmer just below the boiling point for several minutes and remove both again. Season the soup with salt, pepper, and a pinch each of caraway seeds and cayenne pepper.

4 In the meanwhile, clean the fresh mushrooms, rub dry and cut into small pieces. Heat the remaining oil in a skillet over medium heat and fry the mushrooms one portion at a time for 1 to 2 minutes. Turn, season with salt and pepper and add parsley. Add the fried mushrooms to the soup.

"It is best to fry mushrooms in portions. If they can all lie side by side in the skillet, they will cook more evenly. An excellent side dish for the mushrooms in cream sauce – in German called Rahmschwammerl – is bread dumplings (see page 153)."

A. Schuhbeck

Pasta & Noodles

Home Made Pasta

14 oz (400 g) flour and 7 oz (200 g) durum wheat semolina
6 eggs
5–6 tbsp olive oil
salt
flour to roll out dough

4 servings

1 For the pasta dough, combine flour, semolina, eggs, oil and a pinch of salt, and knead until dough is smooth. Wrap the dough in plastic wrap and leave to rest in the refrigerator for about 30 minutes.

2 Roll out dough into thin sheets using a rolling pin or pasta machine while dusting with flour. Roll in pasta sheets. With a knife cut into strips of desired width. The pasta sheets can also be cut with the cutting attachment of pasta machine.

3 Cook pasta in abundant salted water for about 3 minutes until very firm to the bite. Use immediately or mix with olive oil, leave to cool and store in the refrigerator to use later (see below).

Precooking Pasta

1 lb (400–500 g) dried pasta (finished product)
salt
3 tbsp olive oil

4 servings

1 Boil the pasta very firm to the bite in abundant salted water about 4 minutes less than indicated in the instructions on the package. Pour into a sieve and leave to drain briefly. Spread the pasta on a cookie sheet and mix with olive oil. Let the precooked pasta cool off completely. Transfer to a container with tight lid and store in the refrigerator. Pasta can be stored from a few hours up to 2 to 3 days at longest.

2 To utilize, remove pasta in portions from the container and heat up in respective sauce or if preferred in 1 1/4 cups (300 ml) stock. The precooked pasta can be used for all recipes that follow.

"Spreading pasta out on a cookie sheet lets the remaining water vapors evaporate quickly and ensures that pasta stays very firm to the bite. When pasta is warmed up in sauce, it absorbs some of the sauce and gains in tastiness. Sauce should be relatively liquid before heating up because it will thicken during the process."

SPAGHETTI WITH BOLOGNESE SAUCE

For the sauce:

1 onion · 1 carrot · 1 rib celery
1–2 tbsp olive oil
1.1 lb (500 g) ground beef or as an alternative: ground lamb or minced poultry meat
2 tbsp tomato paste
2 fl oz (50 ml) dry white wine
1.6 lb (750 g) canned chunky tomatoes
1 cup (250 ml) poultry stock
1 bay leaf · 2 garlic cloves
1/2 tsp dried oregano
1/2 tsp grated organic lemon zest
salt · freshly ground pepper
sugar · cayenne pepper

For the pasta:

1 lb (400–450 g) spaghetti
salt

Additional ingredients:

3.5 fl oz (100 ml) poultry stock
1–2 tbsp mild olive oil
freshly grated nutmeg
freshly ground pepper

4 servings

1 For the sauce: Peel onion and carrot. Clean and rinse celery. Dice the vegetables finely.

2 In a large saucepan, heat olive oil and braise the diced vegetables over low heat for a few minutes until the onions are translucent. Add ground beef and cook, while stirring, until it is crumbly and has lost its pink color. Stir in the tomato paste and sauté briefly. Deglaze with white wine and reduce the sauce for another 5 to 10 minutes.

3 Add canned tomatoes including juice as well as stock and let the sauce simmer gently for about 2 hours while stirring often. Add bay leaf about 15 minutes before the end of cooking time.

4 When finished cooking, peel garlic, cut in half, and add together with oregano and lemon zest to the sauce. Leave to infuse for 5 minutes. Remove garlic and bay leaf. Season the sauce with salt, pepper and a pinch each of sugar and cayenne pepper.

5 For the pasta: Boil spaghetti according to package instructions in abundant salted water until very firm to the bite, stirring from time to time. Pour into a sieve, drain briefly, and return to the saucepan.

6 Add stock and olive oil to the pasta, mix well and warm up. Grate some nutmeg on top and season with pepper. Arrange on warmed pasta plates and pour Bolognese sauce on top.

Alfons Schuhbeck

"Should you choose to use precooked pasta for the recipe, heat the pasta in 1 1/4 cups (300 ml) broth and season with nutmeg and pepper.
The Bolognese sauce can be replaced with any other meat ragout, for instance, rabbit ragout (see page 58), beef goulash (see page 108) or lamb ragout (see page 118).
Instead of spaghetti, choose ribbon noodles to serve with chunky sauces."

Pappardelle with Rabbit Ragout in Apricot Sauce

For the ragout:

4 rabbit legs à 9 oz (250g), ready to cook
1 small onion · 1/2 carrot
3.5 oz (100 g) celeriac
1–2 tsp allspice corns
1 tsp cinnamon bark slivers
1 tbsp black peppercorns
1–2 tsp juniper berries
2 oz (50 g) dried apricots
5/8 cup (150 ml) dry white wine
1 tbsp oil
2 tbsp brandy
1 tbsp Noilly Prat (French vermouth)
2 1/8 cups (500 ml) poultry stock
1 small bay leaf
1/3 cup (80 g) cream
1 tsp cornstarch
0.7 oz (20 g) cold butter
1 slice garlic
1 strip organic lemon peel
salt · cayenne pepper
a few dashes of lemon juice

For the pasta:

12 oz (350 g) pappardelle
salt

Additional ingredients:

1 tbsp freshly chopped parsley leaves

4 servings

1 For the ragout: Take off the rabbit meat from bones and divide the meat into the single muscle groups. Depending on size, cut crosswise into two or three pieces. Peel onion, carrot and celeriac and cut in very small cubes.

2 Fill allspice, cinnamon bark, peppercorns and juniper berries into a spice grinder. Depending on size, cut apricots into halves or quarters. Simmer five tablespoons white wine in a saucepan for 2 minutes.

3 Heat the oil in a large saucepan, brown the rabbit pieces lightly on all sides over medium heat. Add diced vegetables and braise lightly. Pour in brandy, remaining white wine and vermouth and reduce almost completely. Add stock, cover and simmer gently just below the boiling point for 1 hour. Add bay leaf after 30 minutes cooking time.

4 Strain the cooking liquid through a sieve into a saucepan. Remove bay leaf. Set aside vegetables and meat. Reduce cooking liquid by one third and stir in the cream. Dissolve the starch in some cold water and stir until smooth. Mix into the sauce and simmer over low heat for 2 minutes.

5 Blend the butter into the sauce using a wand mixer. Add apricots, garlic and lemon peel. Season the sauce with salt, a pinch of cayenne pepper, the mixture from the spice grinder and some lemon juice.

6 Gently simmer the sauce for 5 minutes just below the boiling point and then remove whole spices. Return meat and vegetables to sauce and keep warm.

7 For the pasta: Cook the pappardelle in abundant salted water according to package instructions until very firm to the bite, stirring from time to time. Pour into a sieve and leave to drain. Return the pasta to the pot.

8 Add rabbit meat, vegetables and apricot sauce to pappardelle and warm up everything. Arrange the pappardelle with rabbit ragout and sauce on warmed pasta plates and sprinkle with parsley.

Alfons Schuhbeck

"I like to prepare this ragout also with chicken legs. In this case, cooking time is reduced to 45 minutes."

Fusilli with Curry Sauce and Chicken

For the sauce:

1 2/3 cups (400 ml) vegetable stock
1 tbsp mild curry powder
1/2 cup (120 g) cream
0.7 oz (20 g) cold butter · salt
1 garlic clove, peeled and halved
2 slices ginger
1 apple slice, 0.2 inch (5 mm) thick
1 bunch of green onions
4 chicken breasts à 4 oz (120 g),
1 tbsp oil · freshly ground pepper

For the pasta:

14 oz (400 g) fusilli · salt

4 servings

1 For the sauce: Heat up the stock with curry powder and cream in a saucepan. Stir in the butter and season with salt. Add garlic, ginger and the apple slice, leave to infuse for 5 minutes and remove again.

2 Clean green onions, remove the dark green part, cut the white part diagonally into 0.4 inch (1 cm) slices. Rinse the chicken breast, pat dry and cut into 0.6 inch (1 1/2 cm) cubes. Heat the oil in a skillet and brown the meat cubes over low heat on all sides for 2 minutes. Add green onions and season with salt and pepper.

3 For the pasta: Boil the fusilli in abundant salted water according to package instructions very firm to the bite, stirring from time to time. Pour into a sieve and drain well. Return the pasta to the saucepan and warm up together with the curry sauce. Finally stir in chicken meat and green onions. Arrange the pasta with sauce on warmed pasta plates. Sprinkle with parsley to taste.

Truffled Noodle "Gangerl" inside Parmesan Cheese Loaf

2 1/2 cups (600 ml) vegetable stock
1/2 garlic clove
1/2 ginger root
1 oz (30 g) butter
1 tsp chopped truffle
0.9–1 lb (400 g) pasta, e.g. linguini
1–2 tbsp olive oil
1 cheese loaf, preferably parmesan cheese (ideally without any large holes)
freshly ground pepper · salt
cayenne pepper

4 servings

1 Peel and slice garlic and ginger. For the truffle stock, bring vegetable stock to a boil, stir in butter and chopped truffle. Add garlic and ginger. Season with salt and a pinch of cayenne pepper. Remove garlic and ginger again. Pour about 7 fl oz (200 ml) stock into small saucepan. Pour the remaining stock into deep skillet.

2 Boil the noodles in abundant salted water very firm to the bite (cook 4 minutes less than indicated in package instructions). Stir from time to time. Pour into a sieve, drain well, but do not rinse with water. Spread the pasta on a clean work surface or a cookie sheet, leave to cool off briefly and mix with olive oil.

3 Heat up the pasta in the truffle stock in a deep skillet until liquid has been absorbed. Remove lid from the cheese loaf and hollow out in the middle using a fork or ladle. Reserve the removed cheese for later.

4 Pour the pasta with truffle stock portion after portion into the cheese loaf. In between portions, scrape some cheese off from around the edge using a fork or ladle and mix into the pasta. Finally round off the flavor with a pinch of pepper. Serve immediately on warmed plates because the cheese loaf is mostly cold in the beginning. Sprinkle with thinly sliced truffle to taste.

MACARONI WITH MUSHROOM SAUCE

For the sauce:

1 small onion
2 tbsp oil
1 1/2 cups (350 ml) vegetable stock
1 small bay leaf
3 tbsp dried meadow mushrooms
1/2 cup (120 g) cream
0.7 oz (20 g) cold butter, cut into cubes
1 strip of organic lemon peel
salt · freshly ground pepper
ground caraway seeds
cayenne pepper
0.9–1 lb (400 g) fresh mushrooms, e.g. cep, chanterelle or button mushrooms

For the pasta:

12 oz (350 g) macaroni · salt

Additional ingredients:

freshly ground pepper
1 tbsp freshly chopped parsley leaves

4 servings

1 For the sauce: Peel and finely dice onion. Heat a tablespoon oil in a saucepan and sauté the onion cubes until translucent. Pour in the stock and add bay leaf and dried mushrooms. Gently simmer the mushroom sauce just below the boiling point for 20 minutes.

2 Remove bay leaf. Pour in the cream and puree sauce with a wand mixer. Strain through a sieve into a saucepan and gradually mix in the butter. Add lemon peel, leave to infuse for a few minutes and remove again. Season with salt, pepper and a pinch each of caraway seeds and cayenne pepper.

3 Clean the fresh mushrooms, wipe dry, and chop finely. Heat the remaining oil in a large skillet and fry the mushrooms in portions over middle heat for 1 to 2 minutes. Turn over and season with salt and pepper.

4 For the pasta: Boil the macaroni in abundant salted water according to package instructions on package until very firm to the bite, stirring from time to time. Pour into a sieve to drain. Return to saucepan.

5 Add mushroom sauce to the macaroni and warm up together. Finally stir in the fried mushrooms. Season macaroni and mushroom sauce with salt and pepper. Arrange on warmed pasta plates and sprinkle with parsley.

"The best dried mushrooms to use in the sauce are button, meadow or horn of plenty mushrooms. Dried mushrooms develop a strong yet delicate mushroom aroma. I add the fresh mushrooms to the sauce at the end so they stay firm to the bite. According to taste, one can also add one or two tablespoons of the mushroom mixture left in the sieve to the sauce."

Spaghettini with Chili

For the pasta:

0.9-1 lb (400 g) spaghettini
salt

For the sauce:

1 garlic clove
7 fl oz (200 ml) vegetable stock
1 dried chili pepper
2 sage leaves
5 tbsp mild olive oil

Additional ingredients:

2 tbsp grated Parmesan or Pecorino

4 servings

1 For the pasta: Boil the spaghettini in abundant salted water according to package instructions very firm to the bite while stirring occasionally. Pour into a sieve and leave to drain.

2 For the sauce: Peel and slice garlic. Pour the stock into a saucepan and heat up with garlic, chili pepper and sage.

3 Add spaghettini and warm up as well until broth has been completely absorbed by pasta. Finally stir in the olive oil and remove chili pepper and sage leaves.

4 Arrange the spaghettini with sauce on warmed pasta plates and sprinkle with Parmesan.

Spaghetti with Lettuce Pesto

For the pesto:

3 oz (80 g) lettuce leaves
1 tbsp sliced almonds
1 bunch parsley
3 oz (80 g) spinach leaves
salt · 1/2 garlic clove, peeled
1 tbsp grated Parmesan
a few dashes of lemon juice
1/4 cup (60 ml) mild olive oil
1/4 cup (60 g) brown butter

For the pasta:

0.9-1 lb (400 g) spaghetti · salt
5 oz (150 g) cocktail tomatoes
1 tbsp olive oil · freshly ground pepper
3.4 fl oz (100 ml) vegetable stock
grated Parmesan

4 servings

1 Clean lettuce leaves, wash and spin-dry. Lightly toast almonds in a dry skillet over low heat and let cool off. Wash parsley, shake dry and pick the leaves off the stems. Blanch parsley leaves in boiling salted water for 1 to 2 minutes. Pour into a sieve, refresh with cold water, and squeeze water from the leaves by hand.

2 Purée the lettuce leaves with almonds, parsley, garlic, Parmesan, lemon juice, olive oil and brown butter in a blender. Season the lettuce pesto with salt.

3 For the pasta: Boil the spaghetti in abundant salted water according to package instructions very firm to the bite while stirring occasionally. Pour into the sieve to drain briefly. Return to the saucepan.

4 Wash cocktail tomatoes and cut in half. Heat the oil in a skillet and warm up the tomato halves over low heat. Season with salt and pepper. Add stock to the spaghetti in saucepan and heat up. Stir in the lettuce pesto and season with pepper. Arrange the pasta on warmed pasta plates, spread tomatoes on top and sprinkle with grated cheese.

SCHLUTZKRAPFEN STUFFED WITH SPINACH AND QUARK

For the dough:

3.5 oz (100 g) rye flour
3.5 oz (100 g) wheat flour
2 large eggs
1 tbsp olive oil · salt

For the stuffing:

12 oz (350 g) spinach · salt
1/2 onion · 1 tbsp butter
a pinch of diced garlic
5 oz (150 g) quark (curd cheese)
1.4 oz (40 g) grated Alpine cheese or as an alternative: Monterey Jack
1 tbsp brown butter (see page 26)
freshly ground pepper
freshly grated nutmeg

Additional ingredients:

flour for dusting
1 whisked egg white
3.5 oz (100 g) brown butter
2 slices garlic
salt · freshly ground pepper
1 tbsp finely chopped chives
1 tbsp grated Parmesan or Pecorino

4 servings

1 For the dough: Combine both types of flour, eggs, olive oil and a pinch of salt, and knead until the dough is smooth. Wrap in plastic wrap and refrigerate for about 30 minutes.

2 For the stuffing: Pick through the spinach leaves, wash and drain. Remove thick stems. Blanch for 1 minute in boiling salted water. Strain into a sieve, refresh with cold water and leave to drain. Squeeze the leaves with hands to remove excess moisture. Finely chop spinach.

3 Peel and finely dice onion. Melt the butter in a skillet and sauté the onion cubes over low heat until translucent. Stir in the garlic.

4 In a bowl, mix quark with the onion-garlic mixture, spinach, Alpine cheese and the brown butter. Season the quark mixture with salt, pepper and nutmeg.

5 For the Schlutzkrapfen, roll out the noodle dough with a rolling pin or a pasta machine into very thin about 2.4 inches (6 cm) wide pasta strips while dusting with flour. Cover every rolled out pasta strip with plastic wrap. Remove plastic wrap and brush the pasta strips with egg white. Using a teaspoon, place the filling in the middle leaving gaps of 1.2 to1.6 inches (3 to 4 cm). Place another pasta strip lengthwise on top and press firmly around the filling. With the help of a round cutter (2 inches / 5 cm diameter) cut out crescent shaped pockets and press the edges firmly to seal, smoothing out any air bubbles.

6 Heat brown butter and garlic in a skillet. Cook the Schlutzkrapfen in boiling salted water for 2 minutes firm to the bite. Remove with a skimmer and toss in garlic butter. Season with salt and pepper. Arrange on warmed plates and sprinkle with chopped chives and grated cheese.

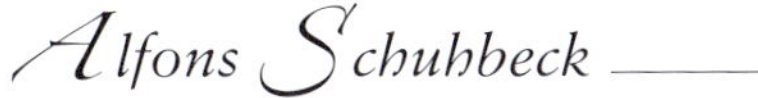

"Like other stuffed pasta, Schlutzkrapfen – a Bavarian specialty – freezes well. Place the raw filled pasta on a little cookie sheet sprinkled with semolina and freeze. Place into a freezer container with tight lid once frozen. Remove the desired portion and place into boiling salted water while still frozen. Cooking time is about 3 minutes."

Nudelfleckerl with Pointed Cabbage

For the Nudelfleckerl (stuffed pasta):

9 oz (250 g) flour
3.5 oz (100 g) durum wheat semolina
3 eggs · 1 egg yolk
2–3 tbsp olive oil · salt
flour to roll out dough

For the pointed cabbage:

1/4 pointed cabbage or young white cabbage
2 tbsp oil
3.4 fl oz (100 ml) vegetable stock
1 strip organic lemon peel
salt · freshly ground pepper
ground caraway seeds
dried marjoram
1/2 tsp mild sweet paprika powder
0.7 oz (20 g) cold butter

4 servings

1 For the Nudelfleckerl: Combine flour, semolina, eggs, egg yolk, olive oil and a pinch of salt and knead until the dough is smooth. Wrap in plastic wrap and refrigerate for about 30 minutes.

2 Roll out the dough into thin layers using a floured rolling pin or with a pasta machine. Using a serrated pastry wheel, cut out triangles with sides 1.2 to 1.6 inches (3 to 4 cm) long. Boil the Nudelfleckerl in abundant salted water for 3 minutes very firm to the bite. Pour into a sieve and leave to drain.

3 For the pointed cabbage: Remove outside leaves and stalk and cut the remaining leaves into 0.8 to 1.2 inches (2 to 3 cm) large rhombuses. Heat the oil in a large skillet and sauté the pointed cabbage over middle heat. Add stock and lemon peel. Season with salt and pepper.

4 Add Nudelfleckerl to the pointed cabbage and warm up for about 2 minutes. Season with salt, pepper and a pinch of each caraway seeds and marjoram, and round off with paprika powder. Remove lemon peel and stir in the butter. Sprinkle the Nudelfleckerl with freshly chopped parsley to taste.

For Nudelfleckerl with radish and black truffle, prepare the Nudelfleckerl as described in step 1 and 2. Clean and peel 14 oz (400 g) of daikon radish and cut lengthwise into quarters. Cut the quarters into 0.1 inch (3 mm) thin slices. Blanch the radish slices in boiling salted water firm to the bite for 4 minutes. Pour into a sieve, refresh with cold water and leave to drain. In a saucepan, heat up 1/2 cup (125 ml) stock and 1/2 cup (125 g) cream and reduce by one third. Add a tablespoon butter and let it melt. Clean 0.3 oz (10 g) of black truffle. Add radish as well as the precooked pasta to the cream sauce and thinly slice truffle on top. Season with salt, freshly grated nutmeg and a pinch of cayenne pepper.

Swabian Pockets

For the dough:

7 oz (200 g) flour
3.5 oz (100 g) durum wheat semolina
3 eggs
2–3 tbsp olive oil · salt

For the stuffing:

2 oz (50 g) white bread (toast)
2 fl oz (50 ml) milk
1 small onion
3 oz (80 g) streaky bacon
1 tbsp oil
9 oz (250 g) spinach leaves
salt
7 oz (200 g) ground veal
5 oz (150 g) bratwurst meat (sausage meat)
1 large egg
1 tbsp hot mustard
freshly ground pepper
a pinch of grated organic lemon zest
1 tbsp freshly chopped parsley leaves

Additional ingredients:

flour for dusting
1 whisked egg · salt

4 servings

1 For the dough: Combine flour with semolina, eggs, olive oil and a pinch of salt and knead until the dough is smooth and firm. Wrap in plastic wrap and refrigerate for about 30 minutes.

2 For the stuffing: Cut the toast bread into small cubes. Soak the bread cubes in a bowl with milk. Peel and finely dice onion. Cut bacon into small cubes. Heat the oil in a skillet and sauté the bacon cubes over low heat. Add diced onion and braise lightly until translucent.

3 Pick through the spinach leaves, wash and drain. Remove coarse stems. Blanch in boiling salted water for 2 minutes. Pour into a sieve, refresh with cold water and drain. Squeeze leaves well with hands to remove remaining water and chop the spinach finely.

4 Add ground veal and sausage meat to the soaked bread in the bowl. Whisk egg and add. Also, add mustard, bacon-onion mixture and spinach and mix everything well. Season the ground veal mixture with salt, pepper, lemon zest and parsley.

5 Roll out the noodle dough not too thin into 4 to 4.7 inches (10 to 12 cm) large pasta sheets while dusting with flour. Cover every rolled out pasta sheet with plastic wrap. Fill the ground veal mixture into a piping bag with smooth nozzle (1 inch / 2 1/2 cm in diameter).

6 Remove the plastic wrap and brush each pasta sheet with whisked egg. Squeeze the stuffing onto the bottom third of each pasta sheet in one long strand. Roll up the filled pasta sheet lengthwise. Using the handle of a wooden spoon, press down on the noodle roll at 1.2 inch (3 cm) intervals to make Swabian pockets. Cut the Swabian pockets where dough is pressed flat and press to seal the seams. Place the pasta squares in gently simmering salted water or vegetable stock for 5 to 8 minutes. Remove with a skimmer and serve (see below).

"Serve Swabian pockets – in German called Maultaschen – in beef stock sprinkled with finely chopped chives as a starter. Or serve with salad as a main course with a topping of butter fried onions rings."

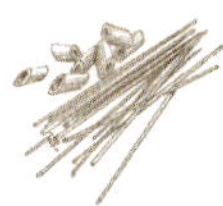

Mountain Farmer Ravioli with Sage Butter

For the dough:

5 oz (140 g) flour
2 oz (60 g) durum wheat semolina
2 small eggs
1–2 tbsp olive oil
salt

For the stuffing:

1.1 lb (500 g) spinach leaves
salt · 1 small onion
1 tbsp butter
5 oz (150 g) cream quark
2 oz (50 g) grated mature Alpine cheese or as an alternative: Monterey Jack
freshly ground pepper
freshly grated nutmeg
1 tbsp brown butter (see page 26)
1 tsp freshly chopped thyme leaves
12 quail eggs (from delicatessen store)

Additional ingredients:

flour for dusting
salt
2 oz (50 g) butter
5 nice sage leaves
1 tbsp brown butter
grated Parmesan or Pecorino

4 servings

1 For the dough: Combine flour, semolina, eggs, olive oil and a pinch of salt and knead until the dough is smooth and supple. Wrap the dough in plastic wrap and refrigerate for at least 30 minutes.

2 For the stuffing: Pick through the spinach leaves, wash and drain. Blanch in boiling salted water for 2 minutes. Pour into a sieve, refresh with cold water and drain. Squeeze leaves with hands to remove the rest of water and chop the spinach finely.

3 Peel and finely dice onion. Melt the butter in a skillet and braise the onion cubes until translucent. In a bowl, mix the spinach with diced onion, quark and Alpine cheese. Season with salt, pepper, nutmeg and brown butter until spicy to taste. Fold thyme leaves into the spinach-quark mixture.

4 Carefully separate the quail eggs. Whisk egg whites. Carefully set aside the egg yolks without breaking yolks.

5 For the ravioli: Divide the dough into four pieces and roll out into four long pasta sheets using a rolling pin or a pasta machine. Dust with flour. Cover each rolled out sheet with plastic wrap. Fill spinach-quark mixture into a piping bag with large nozzle.

6 Remove plastic wrap and brush half of the pasta sheets with a thin layer of whisked egg white. Pipe the stuffing in shape of twelve small rings with 1.2 to 1.6 inches (3 to 4 cm) distance between each ring. Carefully slide one quail yolk into the centre of each ring and loosely place the remaining pasta sheets smoothly on top. Using fingers, press the pasta sheets together around the stuffing. Take care that seams are without air bubbles. With a round cutter (about 3 inches / 8 cm diameter) cut out 12 ravioli and gently simmer in abundant salted water for 2 to 3 minutes.

7 Before serving, melt butter in a skillet over low heat and add sage leaves. Add brown butter and season lightly with salt. Remove ravioli with a skimmer and toss in the sage butter. Arrange ravioli on warmed plates and sprinkle with sage leaves.

Fish & Seafood

Salmon Trout in Salt Crust

For the salmon trout:

1 salmon trout, about 1.7–2.2 lb (800–1000 g), ready to cook
2 parsley sprigs
1 slice organic orange
2 slices organic lemon
fennel seeds
1 small bay leaf
2 slices garlic
1/2 tsp black peppercorns

For the salt crust:

5 small egg whites
3.3 lb (1.5 kg) coarse sea salt
1/4 cup (60 g) flour
1/4 cup (60 g) cornstarch
oil for basting

4 servings

1 For the salmon trout: Rinse the salmon trout inside and out under cold running water, pat dry and cut off fins. Wash the parsley sprigs and shake dry. Cut the orange slices in half and place inside the fish cavity together with the lemon slices, parsley sprigs and a pinch of fennel seeds as well as the bay leaf, garlic and peppercorns. Preheat the oven to 400 °F (200 °C).

2 For the salt crust: Whisk egg whites to soft peaks. Fold in sea salt, flour and cornstarch. Cover a cookie sheet with parchment paper. Use almost half of the salt mass to form a base in size of the fish to place the trout on. Brush the fish with oil and place on the salt mass. Cover with the remaining salt-egg-white mixture.

3 Bake the salmon trout in the oven on the middle rack for about 40 minutes. Break the salt crust open when serving at the table, or cut away a lid using a bread knife. Remove the skin from the trout, take off the fillets and arrange on plates.

Char in Foil

4 chars à about 10 oz (300 g), ready to cook
salt · freshly ground pepper
some parsley leaves
4 small sprigs of fennel fern or dill
4 tbsp olive oil
1 oz (30 g) cold butter
4 slices ginger
4 slices garlic
4 slices organic lemon, 0.2 inch (5 mm) thick
4 bay leaves

4 servings

1 Rinse the chars inside and out and pat dry. Season with salt and pepper. Wash and pat dry parsley leaves and fennel fern. Preheat the oven to 325 °F (160 °C).

2 For every fish, brush one sheet of kitchen foil with olive oil and spread the butter in small flakes. Place each of the chars in the middle of a foil sheet. Fill the cavities with ginger, garlic, lemon slices, bay leaves, parsley leaves and fennel fern. Fold and close the foil over the fish.

3 Cook chars in the oven on the middle rack for about 30 minutes. The fish is ready when the dorsal fin can be pulled out easily. Remove the fish from the foil according to preference and arrange on warmed plates or serve in foil.

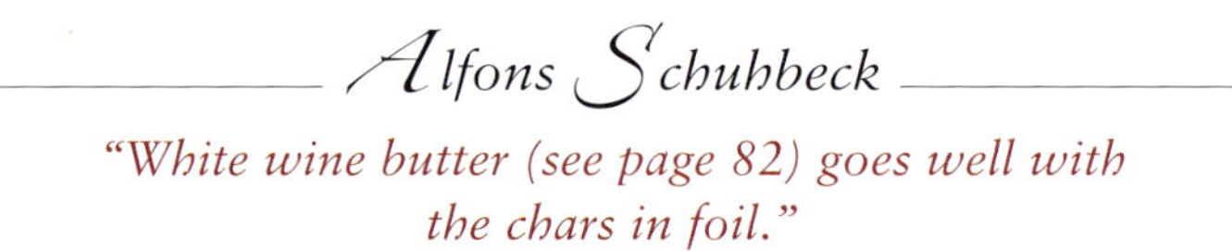

"White wine butter (see page 82) goes well with the chars in foil."

Trout Fillets Cooked in Oven

For the trout fillets:

1 tsp butter to grease
4 trout fillets à about 3 oz (80 g) without skin, boneless

For the herb oil:

4 tbsp vegetable stock
1 tsp lime juice
1–2 tsp freshly chopped basil leaves
a pinch of grated organic lime zest
2 tbsp mild olive oil
salt · freshly ground pepper

4 servings

1 For the trout fillets: Preheat the oven to 210 °F (100 °C). Grease an ovenproof dish (or a cookie sheet) with butter. Rinse the trout fillets and pat dry.

2 Place the trout fillets with the skin side up in the dish and cover tightly with plastic wrap. Cook the fish in the oven on middle rack for 12 to 15 minutes until its flesh appears translucent.

3 For the herb oil: In the meantime, heat the stock in a small saucepan and remove from stove. Add lime juice, basil leaves and lime zest. Stir in the olive oil and season with salt and pepper.

4 Remove trout fillets from the oven and take off the skin. Arrange the trout fillets on warmed plates and drizzle with herb oil before serving.

Poached Trout

4 brown trout à about 10 oz (300 g), ready to cook
1 small carrot
1/2 parsley root
4 oz (120 g) celeriac
1 small onion
1 cup (250 ml) white wine vinegar
2 1/8 (500 ml) dry white wine
salt · cayenne pepper
1 tbsp sugar
1 garlic clove, peeled and halved
1 slice ginger
1 strip organic lemon peel

4 servings

1 Rinse trout inside and pat dry. Do not rinse off the slime that covers the body, it makes the trout go blue when cooked. Peel carrot, parsley root, celeriac and onion and cut into fine strips.

2 Pour about 1.5 quarts (1.5 liters) water, the vinegar and white wine into a large saucepan. Add the vegetable strips, a tablespoon salt, and a pinch each of cayenne pepper and sugar. Heat the liquid until almost boiling. Add garlic, ginger and lemon peel. Place the trout into the saucepan and simmer uncovered over low heat just below the boiling point for about 10 minutes.

3 Carefully remove the trout from the cooking water and arrange on warmed plates. Serve with parsley potatoes and brown butter.

Pan-fried Trout

2 trout à 10 oz (300 g), ready to cook
salt
4 slices garlic
2 parsley sprigs
all purpose flour for coating
4 tbsp oil
1 tbsp butter
1 tbsp brown butter (see page 26)
1 slice ginger
1 strip organic lemon peel
freshly ground pepper
1 tbsp freshly chopped parsley leaves
lemon juice for drizzling

2 servings

1 Preheat the oven to 210 °F (100 °C). Rinse the trout inside and out and pat dry. Salt the cavities and fill with a garlic slice and a parsley sprig each. Put some flour on a plate and coat the trout.

2 Heat the oil in a large skillet and sauté the trout over low heat on both sides. Place the fish on a cookie sheet covered with parchment paper (or in a roasting pan) and allow to finish cooking until still juicy for about 15 minutes.

3 Remove the cooking oil from the skillet with paper towel. Melt butter and brown butter in the skillet. Add the remaining garlic as well as ginger and lemon peel. Leave to infuse for a few minutes over low heat. Season with salt and pepper. Place trout in the skillet, coat with the butter and sprinkle with parsley. Remove all the spices from the herb butter.

4 Arrange the trout on large warmed plates and drizzle with herb butter and some lemon juice.

Lime Oil

1/2 organic lime
5 tbsp mild olive oil
salt · freshly ground pepper

Wash the lime with hot water, dry well and grate the zest. Stir grated zest and olive oil together in a small bowl and season with salt and pepper.

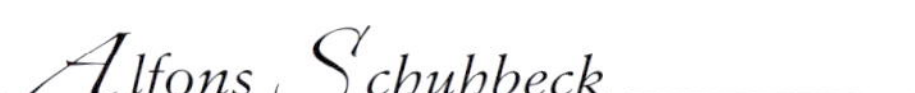

"I like to drizzle the lime oil on fried fish fillets or use it for coating them. It is also excellent with poultry or meat, fried medium rare. To prepare other citrus oils: instead of lime zest, simply grate lemon or orange zest – or a combination of all three – and mix into oil."

Fried Char Fillet on Bear's Garlic Cream Spinach with Roasted Potatoes

For the cream spinach:

10 oz (300 g) low starch potatoes
salt
3.5 oz (100 g) leaf spinach
10 oz (300 g) bear's garlic
1/2 cup (120 g) cream
1 tbsp butter
1 tbsp brown butter (see page 26)
salt · cayenne pepper
freshly grated nutmeg

For the char:

3 Arctic char fillets à about 3 oz (80 g); without skin and boneless
1 tbsp oil · salt
freshly ground pepper

For the roasted potatoes:

1–2 tbsp oil
salt
freshly ground pepper
ground caraway seeds
1 tbsp freshly chopped parsley leaves

4 servings

1 For the cream spinach: Wash the potatoes, peel and cut into 0.2 inch (5 mm) cubes. Simmer the potato dice in salted water for 20 to 30 minutes until soft. Drain into a sieve.

2 Pick through spinach and bear's garlic, wash and drain well, remove any larger stems. Blanch the leaves in boiling salted water for about 3 minutes. Drain into a sieve and refresh with cold water. Allow to drain and gently squeeze any remaining liquid from the leaves with hands. Chop the spinach and bear's garlic leaves coarsely.

3 Heat up the cream. Fill cream, 2 oz (60 g) potato dice, spinach, bear's garlic and butter into a tall container. Purée the mixture with a wand mixer until smooth. Fill puree into a small saucepan, warm over low heat and stir in the brown butter. Season with salt, a pinch of cayenne pepper and some nutmeg.

4 For the char: Rinse the fillets and pat dry. Halve every fillet to obtain eight pieces of about the same size. Heat the oil in a skillet and sear the fillets skin side down over medium heat for 3 to 4 minutes until crisp. Turn the fillets and remove skillet from stove. Allow the fillets to finish cooking in the remaining heat for about 1 minute until its flesh appears translucent. Remove from skillet and drain on paper towel. Season with salt and pepper.

5 For the roasted potatoes: Heat the oil in a skillet and fry the remaining potato dice over medium heat until golden brown. Season with salt, pepper and a pinch of caraway seeds. Sprinkle with parsley.

6 Arrange the char fillets with the bear's garlic cream spinach on warmed plates and place potato dice in a circle all around the edge.

"Should the cream spinach be still liquid, I simply add a few more cooked potato dice and purée well."

Pan-fried Vendace Fillet on Squash Puree with Spice Butter

For the squash puree:

2.2 lb (1 kg) butternut squash e.g. Waltham Butternut or as an alternative 'Muscade de provence' pumpkin
1 garlic clove, peeled and halved
1 strip each of organic lemon and orange peel
2 slices ginger
2 thyme sprigs · salt
1/4 cup (70 g) cream
1/2 tsp curry powder
1–2 tbsp brown butter (see page 26)

For the spice butter:

1 tsp juniper berries
1 tsp coriander corns
1 tbsp black peppercorns
1 tsp small dried chili peppers
1 tsp allspice corns
1 apple, about 5 oz (150 g)
1 tsp icing sugar
2–3 tbsp butter
salt · a few dashes of lemon juice

For the fish:

4 vendace fillets à about 3 oz (80 g) with skin, boneless
1 tbsp oil
salt · freshly ground pepper

4 servings

1 For the squash puree: Preheat the oven to 400 °F (200 °C). Peel squash and remove seeds with a spoon. Cut squash into 0.8 inch (2 cm) cubes and place on a deep oven tray or in an ovenproof dish. Add garlic, lemon and orange peel, ginger, thyme sprigs and a pinch of salt on top and close the tray or dish with kitchen foil. Cook the squash in the oven on the middle rack for about 1 hour until tender.

2 Remove squash from oven and remove all the spices. Place the squash cubes into a fine sieve or cheese cloth and squeeze well to reduce the volume to about half. Purée squeezed squash in blender until smooth.

3 Heat up cream and curry powder together in a saucepan and stir in squash puree. Stir in brown butter and season the puree with salt.

4 For the spice butter: Fill a spice grinder with the juniper berries, coriander corns, peppercorns, chili peppers and allspice corns. Quarter the apple, peel and core. Cut into 0.2 to 0.4 inch (5 to 10 mm) cubes. Caramelize the icing sugar in a skillet over medium heat. Add apple cubes and braise lightly for 1 to 2 minutes. Add butter and salt lightly. Season with the mixture from the spice grinder and some lemon juice.

5 Rinse the vendace fillets, pat dry and cut in half. Heat oil in a skillet, fry the fish fillets skin side down over medium heat until crisp. Remove skillet from stove and turn the fillets. Allow the fish to finish cooking in the remaining heat for about 1 minute until its flesh appears translucent. Remove the fish and drain on paper towel. Season with salt and pepper.

6 Arrange the squash puree on warmed plates, put the vendace fillets on the side and drizzle with spice butter including apple dice.

Alfons Schuhbeck

"Unlike fresh squash, cooked and puréed squash freezes really well."

STECKERLFISH WITH POTATO CUCUMBER VEGETABLES

For the fish:

8 small low starch potatoes
salt · caraway seeds
1–2 tsp oil
4 vendace fillets à 3 oz (80 g), with skin, boneless
freshly ground pepper
5 juniper berries
1/2 tsp coriander corns
1/2 tsp fennel seeds
1/2 yellow mustard corns
1–2 tbsp olive oil
1 garlic clove, unpeeled
1–2 slices ginger
1 tbsp butter

For the vegetables:

0.9–1 lb (400 g) low starch potatoes
salt · 1 cucumber
1/3 cup (80 ml) vegetable stock
1/2 garlic clove
1 slice ginger
salt · freshly ground pepper
1 tbsp freshly chopped dill tips

4 servings

1 For the fish: Boil the unpeeled potatoes in salted water with a pinch of caraway seeds until still firm and strain. Cut away about one quarter to one third of each potato lengthwise. Heat oil in a skillet and roast the potatoes over medium heat. Season with salt and pepper and keep warm.

2 Cut the vendace fillets in half diagonally and place lengthwise on skewers. Season well with salt and pepper.

3 Toast juniper berries, coriander corns, fennel seeds and mustard corns in a skillet without fat over medium heat until fragrant. Crush everything together coarsely with mortar and pestle.

4 Heat a skillet over medium heat and add olive oil together with the coarsed spices. Sear the skewered vendace fillets skin side down for about 2 minutes. Add garlic, ginger and butter. Turn the fish and remove skillet from stove. Allow the fish to finish cooking for another minute.

5 For the vegetables: Peel potatoes and cut into 0.4 inch (1 cm) cubes. Cook the potato dice in salted water for about 20 minutes until done, strain into a sieve and drain. Peel cucumber, cut in half lengthwise and remove seeds with a spoon. Cut the cucumber into cubes of equal size.

6 Heat up potato and cucumber cubes with the stock in a saucepan. Add garlic and ginger, season with salt and pepper and add dill.

7 To serve, place two roasted potatoes on each plate to hold the skewers and arrange the vegetables on the side.

Alfons Schuhbeck

"Vendace is a very good choice for this dish, but can be substituted with char or trout. In Bavaria, Steckerlfish is a very popular specialty. The word Steckerl comes from the Bavarian dialect for little stick."

CARP IN BEER BATTER

For the coating:

1 tbsp allspice corns
1 tbsp caraway seeds
1 tbsp slivers of cinnamon bark
1 tbsp juniper berries
1 tbsp black peppercorns
3 oz (80 g) all purpose flour (ideally Wiener Griessler or wheat flour Type 405)
80 g cornstarch
1 cup (250 ml) beer

For the carp:

1.7 lb (800 g) carp fillet, without skin
salt

Additional ingredients:

1/3 cup (70 ml) clarified butter for frying or as an alternative ghee
1/3 (70 ml) oil for frying
a few dashes of lemon juice

4 servings

1 For the batter: Fill the allspice corns, caraway seeds, cinnamon bark, juniper berries and peppercorns into a spice grinder. Place flour and starch on a plate, mix and season with the mixture from the spice grinder. Pour the beer into a bowl.

2 For the carp: Rinse the fish and pat dry. Cut the carp fillets into 1.6 to 2 inch (4 to 5 cm) large pieces, removing bones with a sharp knife. One after another, salt the fish pieces, turn over in flour to coat, dredge through the beer, and turn once more in the flour mixture.

3 Heat up clarified butter and oil in a skillet. Fry the battered carp pieces over low heat until golden brown on all sides. Remove fish pieces from skillet with a skimmer and drain on paper towel. Drizzle with lemon juice.

"The cornstarch in the batter ensures that the coating fries nice and crispy. When coating with batter, of course it is possible to substitute the beer with wine. The fish dice can also be coated and fried in a classic beer batter, as the one used for the Hollerküchерl (see page 178). Cod or other types of fish are suitable too."

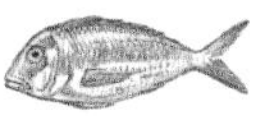

Cod in Bread Crust with Bean Sauce

For the sauce:

7 oz (200 g) small, dried, white beans or 14 oz (400 g) canned beans
1 garlic clove · 1 bay leaf
1 small dried chili pepper
1/3 cup (80 ml) vegetable stock
6 tbsp mild olive oil
dried savory
salt · cayenne pepper

For the cod:

4 cod fillets à about 5 oz (150 g) without skin, boneless
salt · freshly ground pepper
8 slices dark bread, cut wafer-thin (in size of fish fillets)
4 tbsp olive oil

For the marinated herbs:

1 tsp lemon juice
a pinch of grated organic lemon zest
1 tbsp olive oil · salt
freshly ground pepper
0.7 oz (20 g) herb leaves, e.g. parsley, celery leaves, chervil

4 servings

1 For the sauce: A day in advance, soak the beans in cold water overnight. Strain beans next day. Put into a saucepan, cover with fresh water and gently simmer rather than cook over low heat for about 3 hours without lid. 10 minutes before the end of cooking time, peel and halve garlic and add together with the bay leaf and chili pepper. Allow to infuse.

2 Pour the beans into a sieve and remove spices. Put beans and stock into a blender and purée until smooth adding olive oil during the process. Pour the sauce back into the saucepan and heat up. Stir in a pinch of savory and season with salt and a pinch of cayenne pepper.

3 For the cod: Rinse the fillets and pat dry. Season the fillets with salt and pepper on both sides. Place each fish fillet between two slices of bread. Heat olive oil in a skillet and fry the cod sandwiches over very low heat for about 3 minutes on each side until crisp. Remove the sandwiches and set to drain on paper towel.

4 For the marinated herbs: Mix lemon juice, lemon zest and olive oil. Season with salt and pepper. Stir in the herb leaves and if desired, add braised onion dice.

5 Pour the bean sauce on warmed plates, arrange the fried cod in bread crust on top and finish off with marinated herbs spooned over the dish.

Alfons Schuhbeck

"It is easier to slice the bread if it is wrapped in plastic foil the day before. To make sure the slices can be cut wafer-thin, I like to let the bread freeze slightly in the freezer compartment. Depending on the thickness of the fillets and the frying temperature, it can happen that the fillets brown too quickly before being fully cooked. In those cases, they can be placed in the oven for a few minutes at 210 °F (100 °C)."

Wels Catfish Steamed in Vegetable Stock with Root Vegetables

For the vegetables:

1 carrot
1 yellow carrot (can be substituted with 1 carrot)
1 parsley root
1 thin stalk leek
salt
2 tbsp mild olive oil
$^1/_2$ cup (125 ml) vegetable stock
1 tbsp freshly chopped parsley leaves
freshly ground pepper
freshly grated nutmeg

For the wels catfish:

4 wels catfish fillets à about 3.5 oz (100 g), ready to cook
1 tsp fennel seeds
5 juniper berries
1 tsp mustard corns
1 dried red chili pepper
butter for the steamer
salt freshly · ground pepper

For the cardamom butter:

1 tsp cardamom pods
2 tbsp butter
1 scraped vanilla pod
1 slice ginger
1 garlic clove, peeled and halved
salt · cayenne pepper

4 servings

1 For the root vegetables: Peel carrots and parsley root. Clean leek and remove dark green parts. Cut leek lengthwise and rinse. Cut carrots and parsley root lengthwise into very thin slices (less than 0.1 inch / 3 mm). Cut the same slices into 0.2 to 0.4 inch (5 to 10 mm) large strips. Set aside four leek leaves and slice the rest into 0.2 to 04 inch (5 to 10 mm) strips.

2 Blanch the vegetable strips in a saucepan with boiling salted water for 2 minutes. Pour into a sieve, refresh with cold water and drain. Blanch the four reserved leek leaves in boiling salted water for 2 minutes firm to the bite. Strain into a sieve, refresh with cold water and drain.

3 For the wels catfish: Rinse the fillets and pat dry. Wrap one blanched leek leaf around the middle of each fillet. Pour some water into a steamer pot and bring to a boil together with the fennel seeds, juniper berries, mustard corns and chili peppers. Grease a steaming basket with butter, place into the pot and place wels catfish fillets on top. Steam the fish over low heat for about 2 minutes with lid closed. Remove the steamer from stove and allow the fillets to finish cooking for another 5 minutes with lid closed.

4 Heat one to two teaspoons olive oil over low heat in a deep skillet and braise the vegetables. Add stock and cook the vegetables firm to the bite for 2 to 3 minutes with lid closed. Add parsley, season with salt, pepper, nutmeg and drizzle remaining olive oil on top.

5 For the cardamom butter: Toast cardamom lightly over low heat in a skillet. Add butter, vanilla pod, ginger and garlic, season with salt and a pinch of cayenne pepper. Arrange the vegetables on the warmed plates. Season the wels catfish fillets with salt and pepper, arrange on plates and drizzle with cardamom butter.

Fried Pike Perch on Fennel-Carrot Vegetables with Pear

For the vegetables:

2 small fennel bulbs
2 carrots
1–2 tsp. oil
1/2 cup (125 ml) vegetable stock
1/2 scraped out vanilla pod
1/2 clove garlic, peeled
1–2 tbsp butter
salt · freshly ground pepper
cayenne pepper
1 ripe, firm red pear
1–2 tsp icing sugar

For the pike perch:

1.1 lb (500 g) pike perch fillet, with skin, boneless
1 tbsp oil
salt freshly · ground pepper

4 servings

1 For the vegetables: Wash fennel, clean, and separate layers and cut into 0.8 to 1.2 inch (2 to 3 cm) pieces. Peel carrots and cut diagonally into 0.8 to 1.2 inch, (2 to 3 cm) thick slices. Heat the oil in a saucepan, add the fennel and carrots, and braise lightly over low heat. Add stock, vanilla pod and garlic and cook the vegetables firm to the bite over low heat for about 8 minutes with lid closed. Stir in the butter and season with salt, pepper and a pinch of cayenne pepper.

2 Wash the pear, cut into quarters and core. Cut quarters into wedges. In a skillet, caramelize the icing sugar over low heat. Add pears and sauté on both sides until light brown. Mix with the vegetables. Remove garlic and vanilla pod.

3 For the pike perch: Rinse the pike perch fillets, pat dry and cut into eight equal pieces. Heat the oil in a skillet and fry fillets skin side down for 3 to 4 minutes over medium heat until crisp. Turn the fillets over and remove skillet from stove. Allow the fillets to finish cooking in the remaining heat of the skillet until its flesh appears translucent. Drain the fillets on paper towel. Season with salt and pepper.

4 Arrange the vegetables with some stock beside the pike perch fillets on warmed plates.

White Wine Butter

1 tbsp icing sugar
3.4 fl oz (100 ml) white port wine
3.4 fl oz (100 ml) dry white wine
3.5 oz (100 g) very cold butter
salt · freshly ground pepper

4 servings

1 Sift the icing sugar into a saucepan or a skillet and caramelize over medium heat. Deglaze with port wine and white wine, and reduce by one third.

2 Whisk in butter in small pieces portionwise over low heat. According to taste, add a small piece of organic lemon and orange peel, leave to infuse for about 2 minutes and remove again. Season the white wine butter with salt and pepper.

Monkfish with Caraway Seeds on Potato Sauce

For the sauce:

2 oz (60 g) potato cubes (0.2 inch / 5 mm)
1 tbsp carrot cubes
1 cup (250 ml) vegetable stock
1/2 small bay leaf
1/2 small chili pepper
1 slice each of ginger and garlic
5 tbsp mild olive oil
salt · cayenne pepper
a pinch of grated organic lemon zest

For the fish:

1.1 lb (500 g) monkfish fillet, without skin and boneless
1 tbsp caraway seeds
1 tbsp oil
salt · freshly ground pepper

4 servings

1 For the sauce: Gently simmer potato and carrot cubes in the stock with bay leaf and chili pepper just below the boiling point for 15 to 20 minutes until soft. After 10 minutes cooking time, add garlic and ginger. Remove whole spices again.

2 Purée potatoes and carrots with the stock while adding olive oil in a thin stream. Season the potato sauce with salt and a pinch each of cayenne pepper and lemon zest.

3 For the fish: Rinse the monkfish fillets, pat dry, cut into 0.8 inch (2 cm) thick medallions and sprinkle with caraway seeds on both sides. Heat the oil in a skillet and fry the fillets about 2 minutes each side over medium heat. Remove fillets from skillet and season with salt and pepper.

4 Arrange the potato sauce on warmed plates, place monkfish on top and serve with candied tomatoes (see page 22).

Sole with Lemon-Caper Butter

4 soles à about 1.1 lb (500 g), with skin, ready to cook
1 tbsp oil
oil for cookie sheet
3.5 oz (100 g) brown butter (see page 26)
1–2 tbsp small capers
1 tbsp lemon juice
a pinch of grated organic lemon zest
salt · freshly ground pepper

4 servings

1 Dip the tail end of each sole for 5 to 10 seconds into boiling water until the skin separates from the bone. With a paper towel, grasp and firmly pull skin off starting at the tail fin towards the head on each side. Remove fins and heads with kitchen scissors by cutting along fillets. Rinse soles with cold water inside and out and pat dry.

2 Preheat oven to 210 °F (100 °C). Heat the oil in a large skillet and sauté the soles one by one on both sides for about 1 to 2 minutes over medium heat. Place the soles on an oiled cookie sheet and place in the oven on the middle rack for 7 minutes to finish cooking.

3 Warm the brown butter, add capers, lemon juice and lemon zest. Season soles with salt and pepper. Place the soles on warmed plates and drizzle with the caper butter.

Crispy Fried Pike Perch on Paprika Kraut with Pearl Barley

For the paprika kraut:

1 small onion
2 tbsp pearl barley
salt
1 small bay leaf
2 allspice corns
3 tbsp oil
10 oz (300 g) sauerkraut (canned)
4 tbsp white wine
7 fl oz (200 ml) vegetable stock
2 yellow and 2 red bell peppers
1 tsp sweet paprika powder
1/2 tsp black peppercorns
1/2 tsp coriander corns
2 juniper berries
3 green onions
1 garlic clove
2 oz (60 g) applesauce
sugar · cayenne pepper
3 tbsp butter

For the pike perch:

1.1 lb (500 g) pike perch fillet, with skin, boneless
1 tbsp oil
salt · freshly ground pepper

4 servings

1 For the paprika kraut: Peel onion and cut out one eighth lengthwise. Place pearl barley with about 1 quart (500 ml) salted water, half of the bay leaf, the onion eighth and allspice corns into a saucepan and cook over low heat for about 45 minutes with lid closed.

2 Finely dice the remaining onion. In a saucepan, heat up a tablespoon oil and braise the onion over low heat until translucent. Add sauerkraut (if available, including juice) and braise briefly. Deglaze with white wine and simmer to reduce for a few minutes. Add stock and cook the kraut over low heat for 30 minutes with lid closed.

3 Turn on the oven grill. Cut bell peppers into quarters, remove seeds and rinse the bell pepper pieces. Place on a cookie sheet skin side up and brush with one or two tablespoons oil. Grill the bell pepper pieces in the oven on the top rack for about 5 minutes until the skin forms dark blisters. Remove skin and cut into rhombus shapes.

4 Stir paprika powder with a small quantity of cold water until smooth. Fill peppercorns, coriander corns and juniper berries into a small spice bag. Add stirred paprika powder, paprika rhombuses, remaining bay leaf and the spice bag to the kraut and stew another 15 minutes.

5 Wash and clean green onions and cut diagonally into slices. Peel the garlic and cut in half. Stir green onions and applesauce into kraut. Add garlic, leave to infuse for a few minutes and remove again.

6 Pour the pearl barley into a sieve and remove spices. Rinse pearl barley under running cold water and drain. Mix the pearl barley together with butter under the paprika kraut and season with salt and a pinch each of cayenne pepper and sugar.

7 For the pike perch: Rinse the pike perch fillets, pat dry and cut into eight equal pieces. Heat the oil in a skillet and fry the fillets skin side down for 3 to 4 minutes over medium heat until crisp. Turn the fillets over and remove skillet from stove. Allow the fillets to finish cooking in the remaining heat of the skillet until its flesh appears translucent. Drain the fillets on paper towel. Season with salt and pepper.

8 Arrange paprika kraut and pearl barley beside the crispy pike perch fillets on warmed plates.

Gilthead Seabream on Marinated Paprika Vegetables

For the paprika vegetables:

1 large white onion
1.1 lb (500 g) each of red and yellow bell peppers
6 tbsp olive oil
2 young garlic cloves
½ cup (125 ml) vegetable stock
1 slice ginger
1 tsp hot mustard
juice from ½ lemon
salt · cayenne peppers · sugar
1 tbsp freshly chopped parsley leaves
1–2 tsp small capers
dried savory

For the gilthead seabream:

4 gilthead seabream à about 9 oz (250 g), ready to cook
salt · freshly ground pepper
2 garlic cloves, peeled and halved
4 strips organic lemon peel
4 thyme sprigs
2 tbsp oil

4 servings

1 For the paprika vegetables: Peel onion and cut into 0.8 inch (2 cm) cubes. Cut bell peppers lengthwise in half, remove seeds, wash and cut into rhombus shapes. In a saucepan, heat one or two tablespoons olive oil, add onion cubes and paprika pieces and braise for 2 minutes. Peel garlic and cut into slices. Add vegetable stock, garlic and ginger to the saucepan and gently simmer the vegetables at the boiling point for 10 minutes.

2 Pour the vegetables into a sieve and collect the stock in a bowl. Add mustard, lemon juice, salt and a pinch each of cayenne pepper and sugar. Mix into the stock with a wand mixer while adding olive oil in a thin stream. Add vegetables and mix with marinade. Add parsley, capers and a pinch of savory and blend in carefully.

3 For the gilthead seabream: Preheat the oven to 210 °F (100 °C) and place a cookie sheet on the middle rack. Rinse the gilthead bream inside and out. Pat dry and make two or three incisions in the skin on both sides. Season the fish inside and out with salt and pepper. Fill each cavity with a halved garlic clove, a strip lemon peel and a thyme sprig.

4 Heat oil in a skillet and sauté the gilthead seabream on both sides for about 2 minutes over medium heat. Place the fish on a cookie sheet in the oven for 20 minutes to finish cooking.

5 Place the gilthead seabream on warmed plates and arrange some paprika vegetables beside the fish.

Alfons Schuhbeck

"To test whether fish is cooked, pull the dorsal fin from the meat. If it comes out easily, fish is ready. The oven's low cooking temperature ensures that fish remain especially juicy."

Crayfish in Own Stock

For the crayfish:

20 crayfish (alive)
1/2 tsp caraway seeds·salt

For the crayfish stock:

1 rib celery
1–2 onions
1/2 parsley root
1/2 carrots
1/2 fennel bulb
2 tomatoes
1–2 tsp icing sugar
1 tbsp tomato paste
4 tbsp cognac
6 tbsp vermouth, e.g. Noilly Prat
3.4 fl oz (100 ml) white wine
1 quart (1 liter) vegetable stock
1 bay leaf
1/2 tsp black peppercorns
0.3 oz (10 g) dried button mushrooms
1 garlic clove · 1 slice ginger
1 strip organic lemon peel
a pinch of saffron
salt · cayenne pepper

Additional ingredients:

1/2 cucumber · salt
1 tbsp freshly chopped parsley leaves
1/2 tbsp freshly chopped tarragon leaves

4 servings

1 For the crayfish: Place crayfish with caraway seeds for 1 to 2 minutes into boiling salted water. Pour into a sieve, refresh with cold water and drain. Twist off the pincers, crack open using pliers or kitchen scissors and remove meat. Twist of the tails and peel. Make a small cut at the top of the separated tails and remove the dark vein. Cover the crayfish meat and refrigerate.

2 For the crayfish stock: Preheat the oven to 260 °F (130 °C). Thoroughly wash the crayfish shells and drain. Place on a cookie sheet and dry in the oven on the middle rack for about 40 minutes. Remove the shells and chop coarsely.

3 In the meantime, peel celery, onions, parsley root and carrot and cut into 0.4 inch (1 cm) pieces. Wash the fennel bulb, clean and cut into pieces as well. Wash tomatoes and cut into pieces, removing core (not seeds).

4 In a saucepan, caramelize icing sugar over medium heat. Stir in tomato paste and brown lightly. Deglaze with cognac, vermouth and white wine and reduce until creamy. Add vegetables and crayfish shells and pour in the stock. Add bay leaf, peppercorns and dried button mushrooms. Gently simmer everything just below the boiling point for 30 to 40 minutes with lid closed.

5 Peel garlic and cut in half. Add garlic, ginger and lemon peel to the stock and leave to infuse for a few minutes. Strain the stock through a sieve into a saucepan and season with saffron, salt and a pinch of cayenne pepper.

6 Peel cucumber and use a small scoop or melon baller to cut out small balls. Blanch the cucumber balls in boiling salted water for 2 minutes firm to the bite. Pour into a sieve, refresh with cold water and drain.

7 Warm up the crayfish meat with cucumber balls in the crayfish stock without boiling. Serve the crayfish with stock in warmed soup bowls and sprinkle with parsley and tarragon.

"A few drops of nut or argan oil will give crayfish stock a particularly delicate aroma. Crayfish stock becomes a cream soup by mixing in 3 oz (80 g) of cream and a piece of cold butter with a wand mixer."

Fish Burger with Sweet-sour Potato-Leek Vegetables

For the vegetables:

1 stalk leek, only white part, about 3.5 oz (100 g)
1 carrot
1.7 lb (800 g) small low starch potatoes
1 tsp icing sugar
1/2 cup (125 ml) dry white wine
2–3 tbsp white wine vinegar
1 2/3 cups (400 ml) vegetable stock
1/2 garlic clove
5 allspice corns
1 dry chili pepper
1 bay leaf · 1 slice ginger
1/3 cup (80 g) cream
salt · freshly ground pepper
2 tbsp butter
4 cocktail gherkins
1 tbsp freshly chopped parsley leaves
freshly grated nutmeg

For the fish burger:

2 oz (50 g) white bread
2 fl oz (50 ml) milk
1/2 bunch green onions
9 oz (250 g) each of salmon fillet and pike perch fillet
1 egg yolk · salt
freshly ground pepper
1/2 tsp curry powder
1/2 tsp finely diced ginger
1/2 garlic clove, finely diced
1/2 tsp grated organic lemon zest
a dash of lemon juice

Additional ingredients:

white bread crumbs · 4 tbsp oil

4 servings

1 For the vegetables: Clean leeks, cut in half lengthwise, wash and cut into 0.4 to 0.8 inch (1 to 2 cm) large strips. Peel carrot and cut diagonally into 0.2 inch (5 mm) thick slices. Peel potatoes and quarter lengthwise.

2 In a saucepan, caramelize the icing sugar over medium heat, deglaze with white wine and vinegar and reduce to one third. Add potato quarters and carrot slices. Add stock and simmer the vegetables for 15 minutes over low heat with lid closed.

3 Peel garlic and fill into a small spice bag together with allspice corns, chili pepper, bay leaf and ginger. Add leek strips and spice bag to saucepan and simmer the vegetables for another 5 minutes until tender.

4 Remove spice bag. Add cream to the vegetables. Season to taste with salt, pepper and if desired, a few dashes of white wine vinegar. Stir the butter into vegetables. Cut cocktail gherkins in half and mix with parsley into the potato vegetables. Finally, sprinkle a pinch of nutmeg on top.

5 For the fish burger: Cut white bread into small cubes and place into a bowl. Pour milk on top and let the bread cubes soak. Clean green onions, wash and cut into fine rings.

6 Rinse salmon and pike perch fillet and pat dry. Cut the fillets into smallest possible cubes and place into a bowl. Add egg yolk, soaked bread cubes and green onions and mix with hands just until blended. Add salt, pepper, curry powder, ginger, garlic, lemon zest and lemon juice to the fish mixture and mix well.

7 Shape small burgers from the fish mixture with wet hands and coat with white bread crumbs. Heat the oil in a skillet and fry the burgers on both sides for 5 to 6 minutes each side over low heat until golden brown. Remove and drain on paper towel.

8 Arrange the fish burgers with the potato-leek vegetables on warmed plates. Can also be served with potato salad (see page 26), which can be garnished to taste with green onion rings.

Meat

BROILED COLLARED SUCKLING PIG WITH LENTILS AND VEGETABLES

For the collared suckling pig:

1.7–2.2 lb (0.8–1 kg) pork belly from suckling pig (boneless, precooked slab of bacon)
2–3 tbsp hot mustard
salt · freshly ground pepper
dried marjoram
ground caraway seeds
1 cup (250 ml) poultry stock

For the vegetables:

5/8 cup (150 g) small green lentils (puy lentils)
2 oz (about 50 g) each of carrots, leek and celeriac
1/2 onion · 1 tbsp oil
1/2–1 tbsp tomato paste
1/3 cup (80 ml) strong red wine
2 1/8 cups (500 ml) poultry stock
2 slices garlic
1 slice ginger
1 small strip organic lemon peel
1 bay leaf
salt · cayenne pepper
1/2–1 tbsp red wine vinegar or balsamic vinegar

4 servings

1 For the collared suckling pig: Preheat the oven to 325 °F (160 °C). Coat the meat side of the suckling pig with mustard and season with salt, pepper and a pinch each of marjoram and caraway seeds. Roll the meat on the long side and tie together with kitchen twine.

2 Pour the poultry stock in a roasting pan. Place the meat in the roasting pan with the seam side down. Cover the pan and cook meat in the oven on the lowest rack for about 2 hours.

3 Raise the oven temperature to 450 °F (240 °C) top heat. Remove roasting pan. Position an oven rack in the center. Place a dripping pan underneath. Remove meat from roasting pan. Season with salt. Put the meat on the rack and roast it crisp for about 30 minutes, turning over several times.

4 For the vegetables: Soak the lentils in cold water for 2 hours. Peel carrots and celery, wash leeks. Cut the vegetables into small cubes. Peel and dice onion. Heat the oil in a skillet and braise onions, carrots and celeriac lightly over low heat.

5 Add the tomato paste to the vegetables, blend together and sauté briefly. Strain the soaked lentils, rinse off briefly, add and mix with the vegetables. Pour in the red wine and reduce somewhat. Pour in the stock and let the vegetables gently simmer for 20 to 25 minutes.

6 After 15 minutes cooking time, add garlic, ginger, lemon peel and bay leaf to the vegetables. Remove just before serving. Finally, add leeks and season lentils and vegetables with salt, cayenne pepper and vinegar.

7 To serve, remove kitchen twine from collared suckling pig and slice the roast with a sharp knife or electric knife. Serve the collared suckling pig roast with the lentil-vegetable mixture.

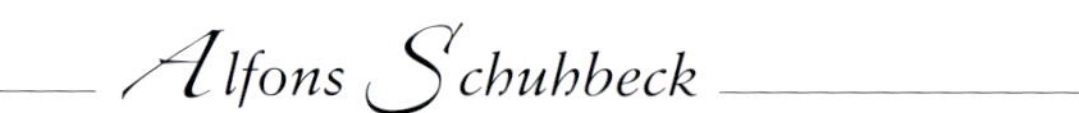

"I only use hot mustard for cooking, because mustard loses its intensity with cooking and becomes milder."

"CRACKLING" ROAST

14 oz (400 g) calf bones
4 1/8 cups (1 l) poultry stock
3.3 lb (1.5 kg) pork belly (precooked slab of bacon with rind)
3 large white onions
1 carrot
5 oz (150 g) celeriac
1.3 lb (600 g) small potatoes
1 tsp icing sugar
1 tbsp tomato paste
1 cup (250 ml) strong red wine
1 tbsp oil
salt
1 small bay leaf
2 garlic cloves, peeled and halved
1 slice ginger
1 strip organic lemon peel
1/2–1 tsp dried marjoram
1/2–1 tsp caraway seeds
freshly ground pepper

4 servings

1 Preheat the oven to 425 °F (220 °C). Spread bones on a cookie sheet and place in the oven on the middle rack. Roast for 50 minutes or until golden brown. Remove and allow fat to drip off the bones. Do not turn off the oven.

2 Reduce the oven temperature to 260 °F (130 °C). Pour half of stock into a roasting pan. Place the pork belly with the rind side down in the pan and roast in the oven on the middle rack for 1 hour.

3 Peel the onions, carrots and celeriac. Cut onions into wedges, carrots diagonally into 0.2 inch (5 mm) slices, and celeriac into 0.4 inch (1 cm) cubes. Wash potatoes, peel and cut either into halves or quarters depending on size.

4 Remove meat from roasting pan and make long cuts into the rind with a sharp knife half an inch apart. Raise the oven temperature to 325 °F (160 °C).

5 Pour the stock out of the roasting pan and set aside. Dab the roasting pan dry with a paper towel and place on the stove over low heat. Add icing sugar and caramelize. Stir in the tomato paste and steam briefly. Deglaze repeatedly with one third of the red wine and reduce to syrup consistency each time.

6 Heat up the oil in a skillet and sauté the vegetables over medium heat. Add to the roasting pan with the browned bones. Pour in the reserved and remaining stock and place the pork roast with the rind facing up on top. Place the pan in the oven on middle rack and roast the meat for 2 hours.

7 Raise the oven temperature to 425 °F (220 °C) using top heat. Remove roasting pan from oven. Place the roast on a cookie sheet, salt the rind and roast on the lowest rack for 20 to 30 minutes until the rind is crisp.

8 Strain the gravy through a sieve into a saucepan, remove bones, place the vegetables in the roasting pan and set aside. If necessary, degrease the pan juices (fat that is swimming on top), add bay leaf and allow the gravy to thicken slightly.

9 Add garlic, ginger, lemon peel, marjoram and caraway seeds to gravy. Allow to infuse for 5 to 10 minutes. Pour the gravy through a sieve back onto the vegetables, heat up and season with salt and pepper. Cut the "crackling" roast into slices and serve with the vegetable casserole and gravy.

Alfons Schubbeck

"Instead of red wine, choose 5 fl oz (150 ml) dark beer or malt beer for the gravy."

Schnitzel with Creamy Mushroom Sauce

1 1/4 cups (300 ml) vegetable stock
2 tbsp dried button mushrooms
8 small schnitzels (veal scallops) à 2.5 oz (70 g)
oil for plastic wrap · 2 tbsp oil
3 1/2 tbsp (50 ml) dry white wine
5 oz (150 g) cream
1 tbsp cornstarch
1 garlic clove, peeled and halved
1 slice ginger
1 strip of organic lemon peel
salt · cayenne pepper
ground caraway seeds
5 oz (150 g) button mushrooms
freshly ground pepper
1 tbsp freshly chopped parsley leaves

4 servings

1 Heat the stock in a small saucepan. Remove from stove. Add dry mushrooms and leave to draw for 20 minutes. Pour into a sieve and reserve the cooking water.

2 Place the schnitzels between two layers of oiled plastic wrap, and pound the schnitzels with a tenderizing hammer until thin. Heat one to two teaspoons oil in a skillet. Brown the schnitzels briefly on both sides, remove from skillet. Pour in the white wine to pan juices and decrease. Add the reserved mushroom cooking water and cream.

3 Dissolve cornstarch evenly in a bit of cold water, blend into the sauce and simmer for about 2 minutes. Add garlic, ginger, and lemon peel to the sauce. Leave to infuse for a few minutes before removing. Season the sauce with salt and a pinch each of cayenne pepper and caraway seeds.

4 Clean button mushrooms, pat dry and cut into thin slices. Heat the remaining oil in a skillet. Add mushrooms one portion at a time and fry for 1 to 2 minutes. Season with salt and pepper, and finally add parsley. Add mushrooms to the sauce. Warm up the schnitzels in the sauce.

Viennese Schnitzel

2 eggs
1 tbsp whipped cream
2/3 cup (80 g) all purpose flour (ideally Wiener Griessler)
7 oz (200 g) white bread crumbs
8 small thin veal schnitzels (scallops from the topside fillet) à about 2 oz (60 g)
salt · freshly ground pepper
7 fl oz (200 ml) oil for frying
1 tbsp butter
juice from 1/2 lemon

4 servings

1 Whisk eggs with cream in a deep plate. Place flour and white bread crumbs into two separate deep plates. Salt and pepper the schnitzels. Coat the pieces one by one with flour and shake off excess. Then dip in the egg-cream mixture. Finally, coat well with the white bread crumbs, taking care not to press too hard.

2 Heat the oil in a skillet over medium temperature. Fry the breaded schnitzels on one side until they are golden brown, then turn. Move the oil around the schnitzels with a light back-and forward movement of the pan so that the batter curves up like a wave. You can also pour hot oil over the schnitzels with a spoon until it is a beautiful golden brown. Finish off by melting the butter in the pan.

3 Take the fried schnitzels out of the pan and drain on a paper towel. Sprinkle lightly with salt and drizzle with lemon juice.

STUFFED CABBAGE ROLLS WITH TOMATO SAUCE

For the cabbage rolls:

salt · 1 head of white cabbage
1 tbsp oil
1 cup (250 ml) poultry stock

For the stuffing:

2 oz (60 g) white bread
3.4 fl oz (100 ml) milk
1/2 small onion
1 tbsp butter · 1 egg
1 tsp hot mustard
grated zest of 1/2 organic lemon
7 oz (200 g) ground veal
7 oz (200 g) ground pork
salt · freshly ground pepper
dried marjoram
1 tbsp freshly chopped parsley leaves

For the sauce:

1 carrot · 1 onion
1/2 garlic clove
1/2–1 tsp tomato paste · 1 tbsp oil
7 oz (200 g) canned puréed tomatoes · 2 slices garlic
1 tsp each of allspice corns, coriander seeds, black peppercorns, slivers of cinnamon bark
1 tbsp cold butter or mild olive oil
salt · sugar · cayenne pepper

4 servings

1 For the cabbage rolls: Bring a large quantity of salt water to a boil in a large saucepan. Remove the hard core from the cabbage. Insert a meat knife into the opening and spear the cabbage. Immerse the cabbage head in the boiling water for several minutes, while peeling off four single leaves one by one. Cut the veins of the leaves flat with a knife and dry off with paper towels. Reserve the remaining cabbage head for other recipes.

2 For the stuffing: Remove the crusts from the white bread. Cut the bread into cubes and soak them in a bowl of milk. Peel and finely dice onion. Melt the butter in a skillet and braise the onion cubes over low heat until translucent. Whisk egg, mustard and the lemon peel together.

3 Mix both kinds of ground meat with the softened bread, the diced onion and beaten eggs. Season with salt, pepper, a pinch of marjoram and the parsley. Fill each cabbage leaf with one quarter of the stuffing. Flatten the long side of the leaves and roll up the leaves from the small end. Tie together tightly with kitchen twine.

4 Heat a tablespoon oil in a skillet and place the stuffed cabbage rolls seam side down in the skillet. Brown the rolls on all sides over medium heat, then remove them from skillet. Remove skillet from the stove and add the stock to the pan juices.

5 For the sauce: Peel carrot and onion and cut into small cubes. Peel and chop garlic. Pour the remaining oil in a deep pan and braise carrot, onion cubes and garlic lightly. Stir in the tomato paste and sauté briefly. Pour in pan juices and puréed tomatoes, place the cabbage rolls in the sauce. Cover and stew over low heat for 30 minutes. Add garlic slices 5 minutes before the end of cooking time, leave to infuse and remove again.

6 Remove the cabbage rolls from sauce. Fill the spice grinder with allspice and coriander corns as well as peppercorns and cinnamon bark. Melt the butter in the sauce and season with salt, spices from the spice grinder, and a pinch each of sugar and cayenne pepper. Serve the cabbage in the sauce.

"When you dip a head of cabbage in boiling water, the leaves become supple and can be separated from the head more easily. Sometimes I wrap a piece of bacon around the cabbage roll before frying it."

Meat Pflanzerl

3 oz (80 g) white bread
3.4 fl oz (100 ml) milk
½ onion · 1 tbsp oil
2 eggs
2 tsp hot mustard · salt
freshly ground pepper
freshly grated nutmeg
grated zest of ½ organic lemon
½ tsp grated organic orange zest
9 oz (250 g) ground veal
9 oz (250 g) ground pork
dried marjoram
1 tbsp freshly chopped parsley leaves
oil for frying

4 servings

1 Remove bread crusts. Dice and soak the bread in a bowl of milk. Peel onion and cut into very small cubes. Heat the oil in a skillet and braise onion dice over low heat until transparent. Whisk eggs with mustard, a bit of salt and pepper, lemon and orange zest and a pinch of nutmeg.

2 Mix both kinds of ground beef with soaked bread as well as whisked eggs, diced onion, parsley and a pinch of marjoram.

3 Form small burger (in Bavarian called Pflanzerl) from the mixture with wet hands. Heat some oil in a skillet and fry both sides of the meat pflanzerl over medium heat until golden brown. Remove burgers from skillet and drain on paper towel.

Szegediner Goulash

2.2 lb (1 kg) pork shoulder, boneless and without rind
3 onions
1–2 tbsp oil
1 tbsp tomato paste
3⅓ cup (800 ml) poultry stock
½–1 tbsp sweet paprika powder
2 garlic cloves
1 strip organic lemon peel
1 tsp each of caraway seeds and dried marjoram
14 oz (400 g) cooked sauerkraut
salt · cayenne pepper
5 oz (150 g) crème fraîche
1 tbsp finely chopped chives

4 servings

1 Cut the meat into 1.2 inch (3 cm) cubes. Peel the onions, cut in half, and then into thin slices.

2 Heat the oil in a saucepan. Brown the meat in portions over low heat and remove from saucepan. Add onions and braise lightly over low heat. Stir in the tomato paste. Return meat to the saucepan and pour the stock over it.

3 Cover saucepan with lid, leaving it partially open to allow moisture to escape. Simmer the meat over low heat for 2 hours, but do not let it boil. Take off the lid after 1 hour so that the sauce can boil down und become a bit thicker.

4 Stir paprika powder with a little bit of water until it is smooth. Peel garlic and chop finely with lemon peel, caraway seeds and marjoram.

5 Drain the sauerkraut in a sieve, stir into goulash and heat up everything. Add stirred paprika and chopped spices and leave to infuse for 15 minutes. Season with salt and a pinch of cayenne pepper. To serve, garnish with crème fraîche and sprinkle with chives.

Veal Goulash with Diced Apples in Cream Sauce

2.2 lb (1 kg) veal (from the shoulder)
2.2 lb (1 kg) onions, peeled
1 apple
2 tbsp oil
1 tbsp tomato paste
2 1/8 cups (500 ml) poultry stock
1–2 garlic cloves
1 tsp ground marjoram
1 tsp ground caraway seeds
1 tsp grated organic lemon zest
1/2–1 tbsp sweet paprika powder
1/3 cup (80 g) cream
salt · cayenne pepper

4 servings

1 Remove fat and heavy tendons from veal and cut the meat into 1.2 inch (3 cm) cubes. Cut onions in half and then into strips. Cut apples into quarters, peel and core. Dice one apple quarter.

2 Heat the oil in a large casserole (Dutch oven). Brown the veal cubes over medium heat and remove. Add onions and braise until translucent. Add diced apple. Stir in the tomato paste and continue to steam briefly. Return meat to the pot and pour in the stock. Cover pot with lid, leaving it partially open to let moisture escape and simmer the goulash for 2 to 3 hours.

3 For the goulash seasoning, peel and finely chop garlic. Mix garlic with marjoram, ground caraway seeds and lemon zest. Stir paprika powder with a little bit of water until smooth. Dice the remaining apple into 0.4 inch (1 cm) cubes.

4 Remove meat cubes from casserole with a skimmer. Stir in the goulash seasoning, stirred paprika and cream. Season with salt and cayenne pepper. Return meat to the pot and add the diced apples. Simmer the veal goulash with cream sauce for 10 minutes just below the boiling point.

Veal Strips in Cream Sauce

2.2 lb (600 g) veal fillet, cut into thin slices · 1 onion
10 oz (300 g) small firm button mushrooms
4 tbsp oil
3.4 fl oz (100 ml) white wine
7 fl oz (200 ml) poultry stock
7 fl oz (200 g) cream
1 level tsp cornstarch
1 garlic clove, peeled and halved
1 slice ginger
1 strip organic lemon peel
salt · freshly ground pepper
1 tbsp freshly chopped parsley leaves

4 servings

1 Cut the veal fillet into strips. Peel and dice onion. Clean the button mushrooms, dry off and cut into slices.

2 Heat two tablespoons oil in a skillet and brown the meat in portions over medium temperature, remove and set aside. Heat one tablespoon oil in the same skillet and braise the onions over low heat until translucent. Pour in the white wine and boil down. Add stock and cream. Dissolve cornstarch in some cold water until smooth, stir into sauce and let it boil gently for about 1 to 2 minutes. Add garlic, ginger and lemon peel to sauce, leave to infuse for several minutes and remove again.

3 Heat the remaining oil in a second skillet and brown the mushrooms for 1 to 2 minutes. Season with salt and pepper. Put veal strips and mushrooms in the cream sauce. Season with salt and pepper. To serve, sprinkle with parsley.

Stuffed Breast of Milk-fed Calf with Vegetable Casserole

For the stuffing:

2 tbsp dried black chanterelle mushrooms
9 oz (250 g) white bread, crust removed
½ onion · 1 tbsp butter
7 fl oz (200 ml) milk
3 eggs
1 tbsp freshly chopped parsley leaves
salt · freshly ground pepper
freshly grated nutmeg

For the calf breast:

3.3 lb (1.5 kg) milk-fed calf breast, ready to cook
salt · freshly ground pepper
3 onions · 2 carrots
7 oz (200 g) celeriac
1 tsp icing sugar
1 tsp tomato paste
1 cup (250 ml) red wine
1 tbsp oil
2 ⅛ cups (500 ml) poultry stock
1 bay leaf
1–2 tsp cornstarch
3 parsley sprigs
1 garlic clove, peeled and halved
1 slice ginger
1 strip of organic lemon peel
0.7 oz (20 g) cold butter

4 to 6 servings

1 For the stuffing: Bring some water in a small saucepan to a boil and add mushrooms. Simmer for 5 minutes. Pour the mushrooms into a sieve, refresh with cold water, drain and cut into small pieces. Dice white bread and set aside in a bowl.

2 Peel und finely dice onion. Melt the butter in a skillet and braise the onion cubes until translucent. Bring milk to a boil in a saucepan. Beat the eggs in a bowl, slowly add hot milk and stir the mixture. Pour the egg-milk mixture over the white bread and mix with mushrooms, onion cubes and parsley. Season the bread mixture with salt, pepper and nutmeg.

3 For the calf breast: Cut a pocket into the meat with a sharp knife and season inside and out with salt and pepper. Stuff the calf breast with the bread mixture, but not completely. Close the open side with either a trussing needle or sew it up. Peel onions, carrots and celeriac and cut into 0.4 inch to 0.8 inch (1 to 2 cm) pieces. Preheat the oven to 300 °F (150 °C).

4 Caramelize the icing sugar in a large roasting pan. Stir in the tomato paste and sauté briefly. Deglaze repeatedly with a third of the red wine and reduce every time. Heat the oil in a skillet and braise the vegetables lightly over medium heat. Pour the stock into the roasting pan. Place the calf breast on top and stew on the middle rack in the oven for 3 to 3 ½ hours. While stewing continue to pour over stock.

5 Remove calf breast from roasting pan and set in a warm place. Strain the gravy through a sieve into a saucepan and reserve the vegetables. Add bay leaf to saucepan and reduce the gravy by one third. Dissolve cornstarch in some cold water until smooth and mix into the gravy. Simmer gently for 2 minutes. Pick parsley leaves off the stems and set aside. Add parsley stems, garlic, ginger and lemon peel to gravy and leave to infuse for several minutes. Remove spices.

6 Return vegetables to saucepan and season the gravy with salt and pepper. Add butter in small pieces and heat up the gravy once more. Chop parsley leaves and blend in. Cut the milk-fed calf breast into slices and serve on warmed plates with vegetable casserole and gravy.

STEWED FILLET OF VEAL HAUNCH WITH VEGETABLE SAUCE

1 onion · 1 carrot
5 oz (150 g) celeriac
2 tomatoes
2.6 lb (1.2 kg) fillet of veal haunch
salt · freshly ground pepper
2–3 tbsp oil
1 tsp icing sugar
1 1/4 cups (300 ml) strong red wine
1 tbsp tomato paste
3.5 oz (100 g) canned puréed tomatoes
2 1/8 cups (500 ml) poultry stock
1 bay leaf
4 juniper berries
1 tsp black peppercorns
6 allspice corns
1 tbsp (10 g) mixed dried mushrooms
1 garlic clove, peeled and halved
1 strip organic lemon peel
2 thyme sprigs
1/8 cup (30 g) cold butter
1–2 tsp hot mustard

4 servings

1 Preheat the oven to 300 °F (150 °C). Peel onion, carrot and celeriac and cut into small pieces. Wash tomatoes, cut in half and then into small pieces, while removing core (not the seeds). Season the fillet of veal haunch with salt and pepper.

2 Heat one to two tablespoons oil in a roasting pan and brown the meat over medium heat. Remove from pan. Sift the icing sugar into the roasting pan and caramelize. Add a third of the red wine and stir in the tomato paste. Reduce to syrup consistency. Deglaze with the remaining red wine two more times and reduce each time.

3 Heat the remaining oil in a pan and sauté onion, carrot and celeriac over medium heat. Add vegetables with tomatoes, puréed tomatoes and stock to the roasting pan and place the fillet of veal haunch on top. Cover roasting pan with lid and stew the fillet until tender for about 3 hours, turning several times while cooking. After 2 1/2 hours add bay leaf, juniper berries, peppercorns, allspice corns and the dried mushrooms to the gravy.

4 Remove meat from roasting pan and keep warm. Strain the gravy and press the vegetables through a sieve into a saucepan. Simmer with garlic, lemon peel and thyme sprigs over low heat. Remove spices again. First blend in the cold butter in small pieces and then add mustard. Season gravy with salt and pepper, slice the meat against the grain and heat up in the gravy. Serve slices of meat with gravy on warmed plates.

"Thanks to the red wine, vegetables will keep their shape even after long periods of cooking. If you would like to serve the vegetables together with the meat, pour sauce through a sieve and reserve vegetables, rather than pressing them through. To thicken sauce, dissolve one or two tablespoons of cornstarch in some cold water, blend until smooth and stir into sauce. Simmer for 2 minutes."

THICK BEEF FILLET STEAK

4 beef fillet steaks à 2 to 2.4 inches (5 to 6 cm) thick, a total of about 1.7 lb (800g)
1–2 tsp oil
flavored butter of your choice, e.g. cardamom butter (see page 112)
salt · freshly ground pepper

4 servings

1 Preheat the oven to 210 °F (100 °C). Place the oven rack in the middle and a dripping pan underneath. Flatten the steaks somewhat with the ball of your hand. Heat the oil in a skillet and brown the steaks on each side over medium heat. Remove meat from skillet and roast on the oven rack for 50 to 60 minutes until medium done.

2 Prepare seasoned butter in a pan and turn the steaks to coat over low heat. Season with salt and pepper.

"You can prepare thick veal fillet steaks, beef rib eye or sirloin steak (0.8 to 1.2 inches / 2 to 3 cm thick) in the same way."

WHOLE ROASTED BEEF FILLET

1–2 tsp oil
1.7 lb (800 g) beef fillet (tenderloin)
flavored butter of your choice, e.g. cardamom butter (see page 112)
salt · freshly ground pepper

4 servings

1 Preheat the oven to 210 °F (100 °C). Put the oven rack in the middle and place a dripping pan underneath.

2 Heat the oil in a skillet and brown the beef fillet on all sides over medium heat. Remove meat from skillet and roast for about 2 hours in the oven on the rack until medium done.

3 Prepare the seasoned butter in a pan and turn the fillet to coat over low heat. Season with salt and pepper.

THYME BUTTER

4 tbsp butter
1 garlic clove, peeled
1 thyme sprig
1 strip organic lemon peel or 1/2 tsp grated zest

4 servings

Melt the butter in a pan over low heat. Cut garlic into slices and add with thyme sprig and lemon zest to melted butter. Leave to infuse for 3 to 4 minutes and remove again.

Whole Braised Veal Shank

2 onions
1 carrot
4 oz (120 g) celeriac
2–3 tbsp oil
1 veal shank, about 6.6 lb (3 kg), ready to cook
2 tsp icing sugar
1 tbsp tomato paste
5/8 cup (150 ml) red wine
2 1/8 cup (500 ml) poultry stock
1 bay leaf
1/2 tsp black peppercorns
1 garlic clove, peeled
1 slice ginger
1 strip organic lemon peel
1 thyme sprig
salt · freshly ground pepper

4 servings

1 Preheat the oven to 325 °F (160 °C). Peel onions, carrot and celeriac. Cut onions into small pieces. Cut carrots and celeriac into pieces.

2 Heat one or two tablespoons oil in a roasting pan. Brown the veal shank on all sides over medium heat and remove. Dab the roasting pan with paper towel to remove fat. Sift the icing sugar into the roasting pan and caramelize. Stir in tomato paste and braise briefly. Deglaze with half of the wine and reduce until syrupy. Add the remaining wine and reduce again.

3 Heat the remaining oil in a pan and sauté the vegetables over medium heat. Place the vegetables in roasting pan and pour in the stock. Place the veal shank on top and put on the lid. Stew shank in the oven on the middle rack for about 4 1/2 hours, turning it over several times. After 2 hours, remove lid and occasionally pour sauce over the veal shank.

4 Remove the veal shank from the roasting pan. Add bay leaf and peppercorns to the sauce and reduce sauce a little bit over medium heat on top of the stove. Allow garlic, ginger, lemon peel and thyme to infuse sauce several minutes. Pour the sauce through a strainer and press through the vegetables. Season the sauce with salt. Cut veal shank into slices, season with salt and pepper and serve with sauce.

"The veal shank will be even juicier if you use the following method: Do not brown the shank, but let it steam for 2 hours. Then caramelize the icing sugar and prepare the sauce with the remaining ingredients as listed above. Place the veal shank on top, stew and finish as described above."

SLICED BEEF FILLET TIPS

1.5 lb (700 g) beef fillet tips, ready to cook
3 tbsp oil · 1 onion
1 tsp icing sugar
1 tsp tomato paste
1/2 cup (125 ml) strong red wine
2 1/2 cups (600 ml) poultry stock
1 small bay leaf
1 garlic clove, unpeeled
1/3 cup (70 g) cream
1 level tsp cornstarch
1 tbsp hot mustard
1/2 tsp rose paprika
7 oz (200 g) small closed button mushrooms
salt · freshly ground pepper
2 oz (60 g) small pickles
cayenne pepper
a pinch of grated organic lemon zest
a few dashes lemon juice
1 tbsp freshly chopped parsley leaves

4 servings

1 Cut fillet tips diagonally into strips. Heat two tablespoons oil in a skillet and brown the meat in portions over medium heat on all sides for about 1 minute. Remove and set aside.

2 Peel and finely dice onion. Caramelize the icing sugar in a skillet. Add onion cubes and braise over low heat until translucent. Stir in the tomato paste, add red wine and reduce until creamy. Pour in the stock, add bay leaf and unpeeled garlic. Reduce the liquid to about one third.

3 Pour cream into the sauce. Stir cornstarch with a little bit of cold water until smooth, stir into sauce and simmer to reduce for 2 minutes. Remove bay leaf and garlic. Stir in mustard and rose paprika and purée the sauce with a wand mixer.

4 Clean button mushrooms, rub dry and cut into slices. Heat remaining oil in a pan and sauté the button mushrooms over medium heat for 1 to 2 minutes. Season with salt and pepper.

5 Cut pickles into fine strips, and add together with the fillet tips to sauce and warm up everything. Season the dish with salt, a pinch each of cayenne pepper, lemon zest and some dashes of lemon juice. Fold in the mushrooms. Serve the sliced beef fillet tips with parsley sprinkled on top.

"Potato-pear puree or Potato-spinach puree (both, see page 156) are excellent side dishes. Instead of beef fillet tips, you can also use pork fillet."

Onion Roast

8 slices top round of beef à about 3 oz (80 g), ready to cook
oil for plastic wrap
salt · freshly ground pepper
2 tbsp oil
3 1/8 cups (750 ml) poultry stock
3 onions
4 tbsp butter
1 tsp icing sugar
1–2 tsp tomato paste
5/8 cup (150 ml) strong wine
dried marjoram
0.7 oz (20 g) cold butter

4 servings

1 Pound the meat slices flat between two layers of oiled plastic wrap. Season with salt and pepper. Heat the oil in a skillet and brown the meat on both sides over medium heat. Remove meat from skillet, pour off cooking fat and pour the juices into broth.

2 Peel onions, cut in half and then into fine strips. Sauté the onion strips in a casserole (Dutch oven) together with butter and icing sugar over medium heat until light brown. Stir in the tomato paste and braise briefly. Deglaze with red wine and reduce.

3 Pour the stock into casserole and bring to a boil. Place the meat inside and stew just below the boiling point for about 1 hour until tender. While stewing, continue to pour sauce on top of the meat. After 50 minutes, add a pinch of marjoram.

4 Before serving, melt butter in sauce and season with salt and pepper.

"If you would like to serve the onion roast – in German called Zwiebelrostbraten – with crispy fried onions, cut onions into rings, turn them in flour, and deep-fry the onion rings in a lot of oil. Drain on paper towel, then salt and pepper. For the sauce, caramelize icing sugar, deglaze with red wine and finish as described in the recipe. Crispy fried onion rings can be an alternative for stewed onions, but are also suitable for garnishing."

BEEF GOULASH

2.2 lb (1 kg) beef, from shoulder or round
2.2 lb (1 kg) onions
2 tbsp oil
1 tbsp tomato paste
4 1/8 cups (1 liter) poultry stock
2 garlic cloves
1 tsp each of caraway seeds and dried marjoram
1/2–1 tsp grated organic lemon zest
1/2 tbsp sweet paprika powder
salt · cayenne pepper

4 servings

1 Remove fat and coarse tendons from beef and cut the meat into 1.2 inch (3 cm) cubes. Peel onions, cut in half and then diagonally into strips.

2 Heat the oil in a large casserole (Dutch oven) and brown beef cubes on all sides over medium heat and remove again. Put the onions into the casserole and braise lightly until translucent. Stir in the tomato paste and braise briefly.

3 Return beef cubes to the casserole and pour in the stock. The meat should be completely covered. Place lid on casserole leaving a slight opening. Stew the goulash over low heat below the boiling point for 4 hours. After 2 1/2 hours, remove lid.

4 For the goulash seasoning, peel garlic and chop finely with caraway seeds, marjoram and lemon zest. Stir paprika powder with a little bit of water until smooth. At the end of cooking time, stir mixed paprika and goulash seasoning into the goulash. Leave to infuse for 5 to 10 minutes and season the goulash with salt and cayenne pepper.

Alfons Schuhbeck

"I use goulash seasoning made from garlic, lemon peel, marjoram and caraway seeds for all types of goulash. If there is any left over, then I mix it with a teaspoon soft butter; that's how you can keep it for several days in the refrigerator.
You can also make the spice mixture for storage. For that, mix the goulash seasoning with butter and fill up a piping bag that does not have a nozzle. Squeeze small piles on wax paper and place in deep-freezer. As soon as the portions are thoroughly frozen, place into a well-closeable storage container."

Beef Roulades

For the roulades:

1/2 small onion
1/2 carrot
1/2 yellow carrot, can be substituted with 1/2 carrot
2 oz (50 g) celeriac
3.5 oz (100 g) pickles
3.5 oz (100 g) smoked bacon
1 tbsp oil
1 tbsp dried horn of plenty mushrooms
2 marinated anchovy fillets
1–2 tsp hot mustard
5 oz (150 g) fresh veal sausage meat
2 tbsp cream
a pinch of grated organic lemon zest
1 tbsp freshly chopped parsley leaves
cayenne pepper · salt
4 thin slices beef à about 5.6 oz (160 g) from the leg
oil for plastic wrap

For the sauce:

1 onion
4 oz (120 g) celeriac
1 carrot · 1 tbsp oil
1 tsp icing sugar
1 tbsp tomato paste
5/8 cup (150 ml) strong red wine
2 1/8 cups (500 ml) poultry stock
1 small bay leaf
1/2 garlic clove
1 strip organic lemon or orange peel
0.3–0.7 oz (10–20 g) cold butter
salt · freshly ground pepper

4 servings

1 For the roulades: Peel onion, carrots and celeriac and cut into small cubes. Cut pickles and smoked bacon into small cubes as well. Heat the oil in a skillet and sauté the bacon cubes over medium heat. Add onions and braise briefly. Remove from stove and leave to cool down.

2 Bring water in a small saucepan to a boil. Add the dried horn of plenty mushrooms and cook for 5 minutes. Pour the mushrooms into a strainer, leave to cool and the cut into small pieces. Chop anchovies very fine. Fold anchovies, mustard, bacon, onion and vegetable cubes as well as mushrooms and pickle cubes into the sausage meat and stir in the cream. According too taste, season with lemon zest, parsley, a pinch of cayenne pepper, and if needed, with a pinch of salt.

3 Pound the beef slices between two layers of oiled plastic wrap with the flat side of a tenderizer. Spread one quarter of the sausage meat mixture each on a slice of meat, keeping the edges free. Fold in the long side of the roulades somewhat, roll the meat together from the small side and hold together with either a toothpick or a skewer.

4 For the sauce: Peel onion, carrots and celeriac and cut into 0.2 inch (5 mm) cubes. Heat the oil in a pan, brown the roulades on all sides over low heat and remove again. Put the vegetables in the pan and sauté.

5 Sift the icing sugar into a casserole and caramelize. Stir in tomato paste. Deglaze with wine and reduce until syrupy. Add vegetable cubes and pour in the stock. Place the roulades in the sauce. Stew covered for about 2 1/2 hours. After 2 hours, add bay leaf. At the end of cooking time, add garlic and lemon or orange peel to sauce, leave to infuse for several minutes and remove again.

6 Take out the roulades and remove the skewer or toothpick. Strain sauce through a sieve, and press through the vegetables. Stir butter into sauce. Season with salt and pepper. Heat up the roulades in the sauce.

Roulade Variations

Ham-truffle stuffing:

5 oz (150 g) poulard breast (roaster), without skin
salt · freshly ground pepper
5/8 cup (150 g) cream
1 tbsp walnut oil
freshly grated nutmeg
1 oz (30 g) marinated black truffle
3.5 oz (100 g) cooked ham
a pinch of grated organic lemon zest

Minced-meat stuffing:

1.4 oz (40 g) white bread
2 fl oz (50 ml) milk
1/4 onion · 1 tsp oil · 1 egg
salt · freshly ground pepper
1 tsp hot mustard
freshly grated nutmeg
1 tsp grated organic lemon zest
a pinch of grated organic orange zest
4.4 oz (125 g) each of ground veal and ground pork · dried marjoram
1 tsp freshly chopped parsley

Bratwurst-meat stuffing:

2 onions · 1 tbsp butter
1 tbsp freshly chopped parsley leaves
a pinch of grated organic lemon zest
dried marjoram
7 oz (200 g) bratwurst meat
1 tsp hot mustard

Chanterelle stuffing:

3.5 oz (100 g) white bread
3.4 fl oz (100 ml) milk · 1 egg
salt · freshly ground pepper
freshly grated nutmeg
1/4 small onion
3 oz (75 g) chanterelle mushrooms
1–2 tsp butter · 2 tbsp ham cubes

4 servings

Prepare roulades with the stuffing of your choice as described on opposite page.

For ham-truffle stuffing: Cut the well-refrigerated poulard meat into small cubes and season well with salt and pepper. Place chicken dice and cream for 5 minutes in the freezer, and then purée coarsely in a turbo blender until the meat begins to bind. Pour in cream in three or four portions one after another and purée all ingredients thoroughly. Each cream portion should be well blended with the meat mixture before adding next portion. Add walnut oil, season with a pinch of nutmeg and set the stuffing in a cold place. Dab truffles dry and cut like ham into 0.1 inch (3 mm) cubes and fold both into stuffing. Season with a pinch each of lemon zest, salt and pepper. Instead of ham and truffle, you can also fold in 4.6 oz (130 g) truffled ham.

For minced-meat stuffing: Remove the crusts from the white bread. Cut the bread into cubes and soak in milk. Peel onion, cut into very small cubes, and braise lightly in a pan in oil over medium heat until translucent. Beat the egg with some salt and pepper, mustard, a pinch each of nutmeg and lemon and orange zest. Mix ground veal and pork with softened bread, whisked egg, a pinch of marjoram as well as onion dice and parsley.

For bratwurst-meat stuffing: Peel and finely dice onions. Melt the butter in a pan and braise the onions over low heat until translucent. Add parsley, lemon zest and a pinch of marjoram. Remove from stove and leave to cool down. Mix the sausage meat with mustard and onions.

For chanterelle stuffing: Remove crusts from white bread and cut the bread into small cubes. Bring milk to a boil, remove from stove and season with salt, pepper and nutmeg. Mix the egg-milk mixture with bread cubes. Peel and finely dice onion. Clean chanterelle mushrooms, rub dry and cut into small pieces. Melt the butter in a pan and braise the onion dice lightly until translucent. Add the chanterelle mushrooms and sauté briefly, mix well with ham cubes, and if desired, with freshly chopped parsley into the bread mixture.

Medium Roasted Beef Tenderloin with Cardamom Butter

For the beef tenderloin:

2.2 lb (1 kg) beef tenderloin, well-hung
1 tbsp oil

For the cardamom butter:

1 tsp green cardamom pods
4 tbsp butter · 1 garlic clove
1/2 scraped vanilla pod
4 fresh small red chili peppers

Additional ingredients:

salt · freshly ground pepper

4 servings

1 For the beef tenderloin: Preheat the oven to 210 °F (100 °C). Place the oven rack in the middle and a dripping pan underneath.

2 Heat the oil in a skillet and brown the beef tenderloin on all sides over medium heat. Remove meat from pan and allow the meat to finish cooking in the oven for 2 1/2 to 3 hours until medium done.

3 For the cardamom butter: Toast the cardamom pods in a non-stick pan without fat over medium heat. Add butter and melt. Peel garlic and cut into slices. Add garlic together with vanilla pod and chili peppers to the melted butter.

4 Remove the beef tenderloin from oven and turn in the cardamom butter over low heat. Season with salt and pepper.

Prime Rib

11 lb (5 kg) prime rib, ready to cook
3 tbsp oil
flavored butter of your choice, e.g. thyme butter (see page 103)
salt · freshly ground pepper

8 to 10 servings

1 Preheat the oven to 210 °F (100 °C). Place a rack in the middle and a dripping pan underneath.

2 Using a sharp knife make diamond shape incisions into the fat side of the prime rib. Heat the oil in a skillet and brown the meat first fat side down and then on all sides over medium heat. Remove meat from skillet and cook in the oven on the rack 5 1/2 to 6 hours until medium done.

3 Prepare the seasoned butter in a pan. Drizzle prime rib with butter and season with salt and pepper.

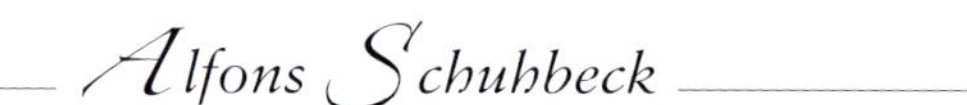

"Instead of fine-grained salt, you can also season the meat with Fleur de Sel, which is a high-quality sea salt that is always sprinkled directly on dishes."

Boiled Beef with Three Different Sauces

For the boiled beef (Tafelspitz):

2 tbsp oil
2.6 lb (1.2 kg) fillet of beef haunch, ready to cook · 3 onions
7 oz (200 g) celeriac · 2 carrots
1 parsley root · 1 bay leaf
1 garlic clove, peeled and halved
1/2 tsp black peppercorns
3 juniper berries
1 medium hot chili pepper
salt · freshly ground pepper
1 tbsp finely chopped chives
1 piece fresh horseradish root, peeled

For the chive sauce:

3.5 oz (100 g) sour cream
1 tsp hot mustard
1 tbsp lemon juice
1 tbsp freshly chopped chives
salt · cayenne pepper · sugar

For the horseradish with bread crumbs (Semmelkren):

3 oz (80 g) white bread
3.4 fl oz (100 ml) beef stock
1 tbsp creamed horseradish, from a jar
1 tbsp whipped cream
salt · cayenne pepper
a few dashes of lemon juice
freshly grated nutmeg

For the horseradish with apple (Apfelkren):

1 apple · 1–2 tsp lemon juice
1 piece fresh horseradish root
salt ·sugar

4 servings

1 For the boiled beef: Heat the oil in a saucepan. Brown the fillet beef of haunch on all sides over medium heat. Pour in about 3 quarts (3 liters) water until meat is covered. Simmer the meat over medium heat keeping the temperature below the boiling point for 3 hours. Skim off foam while cooking.

2 Peel one onion and add peels to stock. Peel celeriac, carrots, parsley root and remaining onions. Cut onions and celeriac into 0.4 inch (1 cm) pieces. Cut carrots and parsley root into slices. Add vegetables to soup after 2 1/2 hours cooking time. Add bay leaf, garlic, peppercorns, juniper berries and chili pepper. Season the broth with salt.

3 For the chive sauce: Stir sour cream with mustard and lemon juice in a small bowl. Stir in the chives and season the sauce with salt, a pinch each of cayenne pepper and sugar. If desired, substitute the sour cream with crème fraîche, yoghurt or schmand (heavy sour cream). Adjust thickness by stirring in more milk or cream.

4 For the horseradish with bread crumbs: Remove the crust from the white bread. Cut white bread into small cubes and soften in cold broth for several minutes. Add cream horseradish and stir all ingredients thoroughly with a whisk. Fold in whipped cream and season the mixture with salt, a pinch of cayenne pepper, a little bit of lemon juice and nutmeg.

5 For the Horseradish with apple: Peel apples, core and cut in quarters. Grate coarsely and mix with lemon juice. Peel horseradish, grate finely and mix with the grated apple. Season with salt and a pinch of sugar.

6 To serve, cut the fillet of beef haunch into finger thick slices, sprinkle with drops of broth and season with salt and pepper. Sprinkle with chives and grate some horseradish on top. According to preference, serve with only one or all three sauces.

"Tafelspitz (boiled beef) is the name of the meat cut which is used to be boiled (a well-hung piece of beef from the rump of a young ox). In Bavaria, this dish is also called Tellerfleisch. Instead of beef of haunch, the flat shoulder or brisket (point half) from beef can also be used. Home fries, bouillon potatoes, green beans cooked with dill, red beet salad, kohlrabi or creamed spinach go along well with boiled beef."

Böfflamott

2 onions
3.5 oz (100 g) celeriac
1 small carrot
2–3 tbsp oil
3.3 lb (1.5 kg) flat beef shoulder, ready to cook
2 tbsp icing sugar
1 tbsp tomato paste
5 tbsp brandy
1 1/2 cups (350 ml) strong red wine
4 1/8 cups (1 liter) poultry stock
1/2 tsp all spice corns
1/2 tsp black peppercorns
1 piece cinnamon bark
5 juniper berries, lightly crushed
1 bay leaf
1 garlic clove, peeled and halved
2 slices ginger
1 strip each of organic lemon and orange peel
2 fl oz (50 ml) red wine vinegar
1.4 oz (40 g) cold butter
salt · cayenne pepper

4 servings

1 Preheat the oven to 325 °F (160 °C). Peel onion, celeriac and carrot and cut into 0.4 inch (1 cm) cubes.

2 Heat one or two tablespoons oil in a casserole and brown the beef shoulder over medium heat and remove. Sift a tablespoon icing sugar into casserole and caramelize. Stir in the tomato paste and sauté briefly. Deglaze with brandy and one third of the red wine and reduce until syrupy. Add the remaining wine little by little and reduce each time.

3 Heat the remaining oil in a pan and sauté vegetable cubes over medium heat. Put vegetables and stock in the casserole. Place the beef shoulder on top. Cover with lid, place in the oven on the lowest rack and stew for about 3 1/2 hours. Turn the meat occasionally while stewing.

4 Remove the meat and set in a warm place. Add allspice corns, peppercorns, cinnamon bark, juniper berries and bay leaf to sauce and reduce sauce by about half. Add garlic, ginger and lemon and orange peel and leave to infuse for 5 minutes. Strain the sauce through a sieve and press through the vegetables.

5 Caramelize remaining icing sugar in a pan over low heat, deglaze with vinegar and reduce until syrupy. Stir pieces of butter into the stew sauce and season with the vinegar syrup, salt and some cayenne pepper. Cut the Böfflamott into slices and serve with sauce on warmed plates.

"For marinated pot roast (in German called Sauerbraten), caramelize a tablespoon icing sugar. Add 2 3/4 cups (650 ml) red wine and 1/3 cup (80 ml) red wine vinegar. Bring to a boil and leave to cool. Marinate meat in the sauce for several days. Prepare the Sauerbraten as you would the Böfflamott, but instead of brandy and red wine vinegar, use the marinade to deglaze the tomato paste. You can also stew with a piece of bread crust or 0.7 oz (20 g) sauce lebkuchen, 2 oz (50 g) raisins, 1/4 peeled apple in pieces. Finally, only stir cold butter into the stew sauce. Add two or three tablespoons cream to round off the sauce."

Stewed Leg of Lamb

2 onions
5 oz (150 g) celeriac
1 carrot
1/2 fennel bulb
3 tbsp oil
1 leg of lamb, about 3.3 lb (1.5 kg) without bone, cleaned and trimmed
1–2 tsp icing sugar
1 tbsp tomato paste
1 1/4 cups (300 ml) strong red wine
4 1/8 cups (1 liter) poultry stock
1 fresh bay leaf
1–2 tsp cornstarch
1 garlic clove, peeled and halved
2 slices ginger
1 rosemary sprig
1 strip organic lemon peel
salt · freshly ground pepper
cayenne pepper

4 servings

1 Preheat the oven to 260 °F (130 °C). Peel onions, cut in half and then into sections. Peel celeriac and carrots and cut into 0.4 inch (1 cm) wide and 1.2 inches (3 cm) long pieces. Clean fennel, wash and cut lengthwise and diagonally into 0.4 inch (1 cm) wide pieces.

2 Heat two tablespoons oil in a casserole and brown the leg of lamb on all sides over medium heat. Remove meat and pour off cooking fat. Sift the icing sugar into the casserole and caramelize over low heat. Stir in the tomato paste and sauté briefly. Deglaze several times with thirds of the red wine and reduce each time.

3 Sauté the vegetables in the remaining oil. Add to the pot with stock and place the leg of lamb on top. Stew on the middle rack for about 3 1/2 hours until medium done. Continue to pour sauce on top while stewing.

4 Take the meat out of the pot and set in a warm place. Pour the sauce through strainer into a saucepan and reserve the vegetables. Add bay leaf to the sauce. Reduce on top of the stove to one third. Stir cornstarch with some cold water until smooth, then stir into sauce and simmer for 1 to 2 minutes.

5 Add garlic, ginger, rosemary sprig and lemon peel, leave to infuse for several minutes and remove again as well as bay leaf. Season the sauce with salt, pepper and a pinch of cayenne pepper. Cut the leg of lamb into slices and serve with sauce and vegetables.

Stewed leg of kid (of the goat) can be prepared exactly as leg of lamb.

Alfons Schuhbeck

"Those who prefer their leg of lamb well-done instead of medium-done should preheat the oven to 325 °F (160 °C). According to taste, cocktail tomatoes cut in half can be added at the end of cooking time. Canned cocktail tomatoes have particularly strong flavor, because they are harvested when they are sun-ripened. Thyme also complements lamb very well and can be used as a substitute for rosemary."

LAMB RAGOUT

1.7 lb (800 g) meat from lamb shoulder, cleaned and trimmed
14 oz (400 g) shallots
1 carrot
1 rib of celery
1/4 fennel bulb
2 tomatoes
2–3 tbsp oil
1 tsp icing sugar
1 tbsp tomato paste
7 fl oz (200 ml) red wine
4 1/8 cups (1 liter) poultry stock
1 bay leaf
2 garlic cloves, peeled and halved
2 slices ginger
1 rosemary sprig
1 strip organic lemon peel
0.7 oz (20 g) cold butter
salt · freshly ground pepper
cayenne pepper

4 servings

1 Cut the lamb shoulder into 1.2 inch (3 cm) cubes. Peel shallots and carrot. Cut shallots into quarters and carrot into slices. Clean and wash celery rib and fennel. Cut celery diagonally into 0.2 inch (5 mm) thick slices, the fennel into 0.4 to 0.8 inch (1 to 2 cm) pieces. Make a shallow incision crosswise on bottom of the tomatoes, blanch, rinse off with cold water, skin, cut into quarters, core and dice.

2 Heat one or two tablespoons oil in a casserole (Dutch oven). Brown the lamb cubes in oil one portion at a time and remove. Sift the icing sugar into casserole and caramelize. Stir in the tomato paste and braise briefly. Pour in half of the red wine and reduce until syrupy. Add remaining red wine and reduce again.

3 Heat the remaining oil in a skillet. Braise shallots, carrot, celery and fennel in the oil over medium heat. Add vegetables to the meat cubes in the pot. Pour stock on top and cover with lid leaving a small crack open. Stew the lamb ragout over low heat for 2 hours. Remove lid after 1 1/2 hours cooking time and add bay leaf.

4 Shortly before the end of cooking time, fold in the tomato cubes. Add garlic, ginger, rosemary sprig and lemon peel to the sauce, leave to infuse for several minutes and remove all seasonings including bay leaf again. Melt butter in the sauce and season the lamb ragout with salt, pepper and a pinch of cayenne pepper.

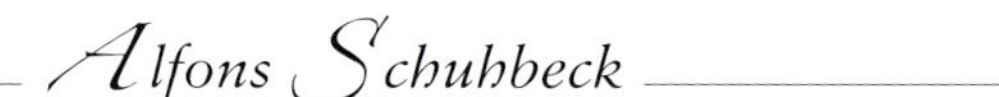

"I serve lamb ragout with either lime rice or cooked potatoes (see page 158). According to taste, substitute the rosemary sprig with thyme."

Cooked Lamb Shoulder

1 lamb shoulder, about 2.6 lb (1.2 kg), without bone, cleaned and trimmed
2 tbsp oil
2–3 quarts (2–3 liters) poultry stock
2 low starch potatoes
1 carrot
5 oz (150 g) celeriac
1 onion
5 allspice corns
1 bay leaf
1 thyme sprig
1 small dried chili pepper
2 garlic cloves, peeled
1 strip organic lemon peel
salt · freshly ground pepper

4 servings

1 Tie the lamb shoulder together with kitchen twine. Heat the oil in a large saucepan and brown the lamb shoulder on all sides over medium heat. Add enough stock to cover the meat. Let the lamb shoulder gently simmer just below the boiling point for 2 hours. Skim off foam.

2 Peel potatoes, carrot, celeriac and onion. Cut potatoes in half lengthwise and crosswise into 0.4 inch (1 cm) thick slices. Cut carrot diagonally into 0.4 inch (1 cm) thick slices. Cut celeriac and onion into 0.4 to 0.8 inch (1 to 2 cm) pieces.

3 Fill the allspice corns into a small spice bag and add to stock together with bay leaf, thyme sprig, chili pepper and vegetables 20 minutes before the end of cooking time. Shortly before the end of cooking time, add garlic and lemon peel and leave to infuse for several minutes.

4 Remove the lamb shoulder from the broth. Strain the broth through a sieve into a pot. Season the broth with salt and pepper. Take off the kitchen twine and cut meat into slices. Serve the lamb shoulder with vegetables and some broth in warmed soup bowls.

Medium-done Saddle of Lamb

1.1 lb (500 g) saddle of lamb fillet, in pieces
1–2 tsp oil
flavored butter of choice, e.g. thyme butter (see page 103)
salt · freshly ground pepper

4 servings

1 Preheat the oven to 210°F (100°C). Place an oven rack in the middle and a dripping pan underneath.

2 Cut the saddle of lamb fillet crosswise. Heat the oil in a pan and brown the meat over medium heat. Remove meat from pan, place on the oven rack, and cook until medium-done for 40 minutes.

3 Prepare the seasoned butter in a pan, turn fillet to coat over low heat and season with salt and pepper.

Poultry & Game

CHICKEN BREAST STRIPS

1.1 lb (500 g) fillets of chicken breast, without skin, ready to cook
1 tbsp oil
1 tbsp butter
salt · freshly ground pepper
1 tbsp freshly chopped parsley leaves

4 servings

1 Rinse the fillets of chicken breast and pat dry. Cut the fillets in half lengthwise and cut long diagonal stripes.

2 Heat the oil in a large skillet and sauté the chicken breast strips over medium heat in two separate portions for about 2 minutes. Drain and set aside.

3 Melt the butter in the skillet. Season with salt and pepper and add parsley. Stir in the sautéed chicken meat and coat with the herbal butter.

"For even more tender meat, do not fry in the skillet, but place strips for 2 minutes into hot salted water at 190 °F (90 °C). Drain well and simply toss in olive oil or herbal butter or add to mustard sauce (see below)."

MUSTARD SAUCE

3.4 fl oz (100 ml) clear vegetable stock
3.4 fl oz (100 g) cream
1 tbsp each of hot and sweet mustard
0.3 oz (10 g) cold butter
salt · cayenne pepper

For about 7 fl oz (200 ml) of sauce

Using a saucepan, bring stock and cream to a boil. Stir in hot and mild mustard. Add butter and allow to melt. Season with salt and a pinch of cayenne pepper.

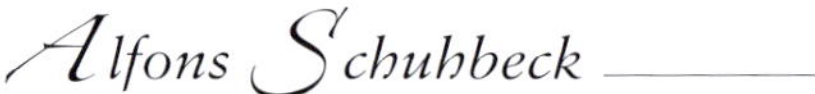

"Mustard sauce is excellent served with medium rare meat, chicken breast, meat cut into strips, boiled beef and fish. Its flavor can be refined by adding some grated zest of an organic lemon or lime, or finely chopped herbs like tarragon or dill. With grated orange zest, it is the perfect accompaniment to fried duck breast."

HERB CHICKEN

1 broiler chicken 2.6–3.1 lb (1.2–1.4 kg)
1 hand full of fresh herb leaves, e.g. sage, basil, parsley, thyme
1 tbsp black peppercorns
1 tbsp allspice corns
1/2 small onion
1/2 apple
1 1/2 organic lemon
1/2 tsp marjoram
1 bay leaf
salt
oil for the cookie sheet
6 parsley sprigs
2 rosemary sprigs
6 garlic cloves, unpeeled
2 oz (50 g) melted butter for basting

4 servings

1 Rinse the chicken inside and out with cold water and pat dry. Lift the skin of the chicken breast and legs using the back of a tablespoon. Place the herb leaves onto meat and pull the skin back on top tightly.

2 Fill the peppercorns and allspice corns into a spice grinder. Peel onion. Wash the apple and core. Wash the half lemon under hot water and dry well. Cut onion, apple and lemon into 0.8 to 1.2 inch (2 to 3 cm) pieces and put into a bowl. Add marjoram and bay leaf. Season the lemon stuffing with salt and spice mixture (from the spice grinder) and mix well. Place the stuffing in the cavity. Grease the oven cookie sheet with oil and preheat the oven to 325 °F (160 °C).

3 Wash the whole lemon with hot water, dry and cut into slices. Wash parsley and rosemary sprigs and shake dry. Place lemon slices, parsley sprigs, rosemary sprigs and garlic on the cookie sheet. Baste the stuffed chicken with butter and place on the cookie sheet as well.

4 Bake the chicken on the lowest rack in the oven for about 1 hour. Baste from time to time with liquid butter. Increase oven temperature to 400 °F (200 °C) and bake the chicken for another 15 to 20 minutes until nice and crispy brown.

5 Cut the herb chicken into portions and arrange on warmed plates. Season lightly to taste with salt and pepper and drizzle with the gravy from the cookie sheet.

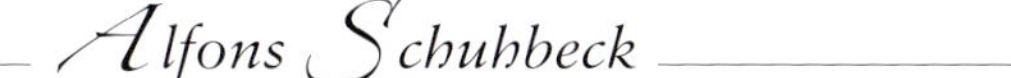

"Mixing one tablespoon of mild olive oil into gravy at the end will highlight their delicate flavor. Herb chicken goes well with crunchy baguette."

Lemon Breaded Fried Chicken

2 eggs
3 tsp lemon juice
freshly ground pepper
freshly grated nutmeg
grated zest of 1 organic lemon
1 tbsp lightly whipped cream
3 oz (80 g) all purpose flour (ideally Wiener Griessler)
3.5 oz (100 g) white bread crumbs
4 chicken breast fillets à 4 oz (120 g), without skin, ready to cook
salt
about 7 fl oz (200 ml) oil for frying
0.3 oz (10 g) cold butter

4 servings

1 Whisk eggs in a deep plate and season with one tablespoon lemon juice, pepper, nutmeg and half of the lemon zest. Fold in the cream. Place flour and white bread crumbs into two separate deep plates.

2 Rinse the chicken breast fillets and pat dry. Cut each chicken breast diagonally into four slices. Season with salt and pepper. First, coat chicken pieces one by one with flour, dip into the egg mixture and finally coat well with the white bread crumbs, taking care not to press too firmly.

3 Pour 0.8 inch (2 cm) of oil into a deep frying pan and heat to medium heat. Fry the breaded chicken pieces until golden brown on both sides. In a second frying pan, melt butter, add the remaining lemon zest and lemon juice. Season with salt and pepper. Briefly turn the chicken pieces in the lemon butter. Serve with lemon wedges and potato salad (see page 26) and garnish with fried parsley sprigs as desired.

"Instead of chicken breast, boneless chicken thighs cut into smaller pieces can also be used. Particularly tender and visually appealing are spring chicken legs. First, remove the skin. Then, using a small sharp knife, remove the thigh bone and partly release the meat from the drumstick before breading. The flavor for the white bread crumbs can be varied by adding spices (for instance, freshly ground pepper with allspice) or chopped herbs (for instance thyme)."

Crunchy Fried Chicken Breasts

4 chicken breasts à about 4 oz (120 g) with skin, ready to cook
1 tbsp oil
flavored butter of choice, e.g. thyme butter (see page 103)
salt · freshly ground pepper

4 servings

1 Preheat the oven to 210 °F (100 °C). Position an oven rack in the center of the oven and place a dripping pan or cookie sheet underneath. Rinse the chicken breasts and pat dry well. Using the oil, fry chicken breasts with skin facing down for about 3 minutes in the frying pan at medium heat until crisp. Turn over and continue frying briefly. Remove chicken breasts from pan and place on the oven rack to finish cooking slowly for 30 to 40 minutes until done and juicy.

2 Prepare the flavored butter in a skillet. Season the chicken breasts with salt and pepper and coat with the butter.

For Guinea fowl breasts: Prepare the breasts as above and cook for 25 to 30 minutes in the oven.

Braised Turkey Leg

2 onions
1 carrot
1 rib of celery
2 turkey legs à about 1.1 lb (500g), with skin, ready to cook
2 tbsp oil
1 tbsp icing sugar
1 tbsp tomato paste
3.4 fl oz (100 ml) dry white wine
1 1/2 cups (350 ml) poultry stock
2 oz (50 g) liquid butter for basting
salt · oil for cookie sheet
1 bay leaf
1 garlic clove, peeled and halved
1 strip organic lemon peel
2 thyme sprigs
freshly ground pepper

4 servings

1 Preheat the oven to 325 °F (160 °C). Peel and finely dice onions and carrot. Wash and clean the celery and cut into small cubes as well. Rinse the turkey legs and pat dry.

2 Heat oil in a large roasting pan (or Dutch oven) and brown the turkey legs on all sides. Remove and set aside. Dust the icing sugar into roasting pan and caramelize. Stir in the tomato paste, deglaze with white wine, and simmer until reduced to syrupy consistency.

3 Heat the remaining oil in a pan and braise the diced carrot, onion and celery. Add vegetable mixture to the roasting pan and pour in the stock. Place the turkey legs on the vegetables. Season the liquid butter with salt and baste the turkey legs. Cook in the oven on the middle rack for 1 1/2 to 2 hours, basting the turkey legs occasionally with the liquid butter.

4 Remove roasting pan from oven. Place the turkey legs on a greased cookie sheet and put them back in the oven. Switch oven to top heat at 400 to 425 °F (200 to 220 °C) and brown the turkey legs for 5 to 10 minutes.

5 Add the bay leaf to the roasting pan and simmer the gravy on the stove until reduced by one third. Add garlic, lemon peel and thyme sprigs and leave to infuse for a few minutes. Then remove together with the bay leaf. Season the sauce with salt and pepper. Arrange the turkey legs with the sauce on warmed plates.

Roasted Turkey

For the sauce:

2 onions · 1 carrot
5 oz (150 g) celeriac
1 tbsp oil
1–2 tsp icing sugar
1/2–1 tbsp tomato paste
1 cup (250 ml) strong red wine
3 1/8 cups (750 ml) poultry stock
1 bay leaf
1/2–1 tsp cornstarch
1 garlic clove, peeled and halved
1 slice of ginger
1 strip of organic lemon peel
1 rosemary sprig
0.3 oz (10 g) cold butter

For the turkey:

1 onion · 1 tbsp oil
4 oz (120 g) cooked ham
1 apple · 2 carrots
10 oz (300 g) white bread, from the day before
1 1/2 cups (350 ml) milk
4 eggs · salt
freshly ground pepper
freshly grated nutmeg
2 oz (50 g) semolina or durum wheat semolina
5 oz (150 g) corn (frozen or canned)
2 oz (50 g) raisins
1 small turkey, about 6.6 lb (3 kg)
3.5 oz (100 g) liquid butter for basting

8 to 10 servings

1 For the sauce: Peel onions, carrot and celeriac and cut into about 0.4 inch (1 cm) cubes. Heat oil in a skillet and braise the vegetable dice for a few minutes.

2 Caramelize the icing sugar lightly over low heat in a saucepan. Stir in the tomato paste and brown lightly. Deglaze with half of the red wine and reduce until creamy. Add the remaining red wine and reduce again. Add the stock and transfer contents to a large roasting pan or a deep cookie sheet. Add the diced vegetables. Preheat the oven to 300 °F (150 °C).

3 For the turkey: Peel and finely dice onion. Heat the oil in a skillet and braise the onion dice until translucent. Dice the ham finely. Peel the apple, cut into quarters and core. Cut into small cubes as well. Clean the carrots, peel and cut into 0.2 inch (5 mm) cubes.

4 Cut the white bread into 0.2 to 0.4 inch (5 to 10 mm) cubes. In a saucepan, bring the milk to a boil and remove from stove. Whisk eggs into milk and season with salt, pepper and nutmeg. Soak the bread cubes in the egg-milk mixture. Mix in the diced onion, ham, apple and carrots as well as semolina, corn and raisins. Season the stuffing one more time, cover and leave to infuse for 10 minutes.

5 Remove the innards from the turkey. Rinse the turkey inside and out and pat dry. Season the cavity with salt. Fill the cavity with the stuffing and close with skewers. Tie the legs together with kitchen twine. Place the turkey, breast side up, in the roasting pan or cookie sheet on top of the sauce and the vegetables. Season the liquid butter with salt and baste the turkey. Cook the turkey on the lowest rack in the oven for 4 1/2 to 5 hours, basting from time to time. Add the bay leaf for the final 15 minutes of cooking time.

6 Remove turkey from the oven und keep warm. Strain the vegetables and the gravy from the roasting pan through a sieve into a saucepan. Dissolve cornstarch in a bit of cold water until smooth, stir into the sauce and simmer for 2 minutes. Add the garlic, ginger, lemon peel and rosemary sprig and leave to infuse for a few minutes, then remove again together with the bay leaf. Stir in the butter and season the sauce with salt and pepper.

Roasted Duck

For the duck:

1/2 onion
1 1/2 apple
salt · freshly ground pepper
dried marjoram
1 farmer's duck, about 5.5 oz (2.5 kg)
5 cups (1.2 liter) poultry stock

For the sauce:

2 onions
1 small carrot
3.5 oz (100 g) celeriac
1 tbsp oil
2 tsp icing sugar
1 tbsp tomato paste
1 cup (250 ml) strong red wine
1 tsp cornstarch
1 marjoram sprig
2 parsley sprigs
2 slices each of ginger and garlic
2 strips organic orange peel
0.7 oz (20 g) cold butter

4 servings

1 For the duck: Preheat the oven to 275 °F (140 °C). Peel and coarsely dice onion. Wash the apple, quarter, core and chop coarsely as well. Mix the apple and onion pieces and season with salt, pepper and a pinch of marjoram. Cut the wings off the duck and remove innards. Rinse the duck inside and out and pat dry.

2 Stuff the duck's cavity with the apple-onion mixture. Place the duck, breast side up, in a roasting pan and add wings. Pour in the stock. Cook duck in covered pan on the lowest rack in the oven for about 3 1/2 hours until skin is light and meat tender. While cooking, skim off fat from time to time and reserve. Remove duck from roasting pan and set aside. Degrease the stock to a large extent and reserve for the sauce.

3 Increase the oven temperature to 425 °F (220 °C). Carefully remove the duck breasts and legs and remove the thigh bone from the legs. Remove the stuffing from the cavity. Using poultry shears or a cleaver, cut the duck carcass into pieces and place them on a cookie sheet. Roast in the oven on the middle rack for about 20 minutes until brown and crisp. Skim off any fat.

4 For the sauce: Peel onions, carrot and celeriac and cut into about 0.4 inch (1 cm) cubes. Heat oil in a skillet and braise the vegetables. Caramelize the icing sugar in a saucepan over low heat. Stir in the tomato paste and brown lightly. Add half of the red wine and reduce to syrupy consistency. Add the remaining red wine and reduce again. Stir in browned bones, braised vegetables and reserved broth, reserving five tablespoons of broth. Simmer just below the boiling point for 1 hour.

5 Strain the sauce through a fine sieve into a saucepan and reduce by half. Dissolve the starch in a bit of cold water and stir into the sauce. Simmer for 2 minutes. Add marjoram sprigs, parsley sprigs, ginger, garlic and orange peel, leave to infuse briefly and remove again. Stir the butter and some of the reserved duck dripping into the sauce. Season with salt.

6 Turn on the oven grill. Place the duck breasts and legs with the skin facing up on a cookie sheet and add the remaining five tablespoons of broth. Cook the duck meat in the oven on the lower rack for 10 to 15 minutes until crisp. Arrange the duck breasts and legs with the sauce on warmed plates. The roasted duck goes well with pretzel dumplings (see page 153), potato dumplings (see page 152), chocolate flavored red cabbage (see page 145) and savoy cabbage with horseradish (see page 150).

Broiled Duck Legs

4 duck legs à 12–14 oz (350–400 g), with skin, ready to cook
1 small onion
1 bay leaf · 3 cloves
4 quarts (4 liters) poultry stock

4 servings

1 Rinse the duck legs and pat dry. Remove thigh bone using a sharp knife. Peel the onion, place the bay leaf on top and hold in place by spiking the onion with cloves. Bring the stock to a boil in a large sauce pan and add the spiked onion and the duck legs. Cook the legs in the broth just below the boiling point for 2 1/2 to 3 hours until tender.

2 Turn on the grill of the oven (broiler). Remove duck legs from broth and place, skin side up, in a deep cookie sheet or a suitable ovenproof container. Add five tablespoons of the broth and broil the duck legs in the oven on the lowest rack for 15 to 20 minutes until crisp.

Roasted Barbarie Duck Breast

4 Barbarie duck breasts à about 7 oz (200 g), with skin
2 tbsp oil
salt · freshly ground pepper

4 servings

1 Preheat the oven to 210 °F (100 °C). Place the oven rack in the middle of the oven with a dripping pan underneath. Rinse the duck breasts and pat dry. Carefully remove fat and tendons. Remove any remaining feathers and quills with tweezers. Using a sharp knife, score the skin of each duck breast, without cutting through to the flesh, in a diamond-shaped pattern.

2 Heat the oil in a skillet and sauté the duck breasts, skin side down, at medium heat for about 5 minutes. Turn over onto meat side and fry for another minute to close pores. Remove duck breasts from skillet and transfer to the oven. Allow to sit on the oven rack for 1 hour.

3 Remove duck breasts from oven. Season with salt and pepper.

"Be sure to really cut the duck skin completely until the edge. This will avoid that the meat bulges while cooking. Duck breast can be served with orange oil: Blend four or three tablespoons of mild olive oil with some grated zest of an organic orange. Add three slices each of ginger and garlic and let infuse for 5 minutes. Drizzle oil on top of the fried duck breast."

STUFFED GOOSE

For the goose:

1 goose, about 10 lb (4.5 kg)
9 oz (250 g) pretzel sticks, from the day before, salt removed
1 cup (250 ml) milk
2 eggs · salt
freshly ground pepper
freshly grated nutmeg
1/2 onion
3.5 oz (100 g) butter
9 oz (250 g) bratwurst sausage meat
5 tbsp cream
1 tbsp freshly chopped parsley leaves
1–2 tsp grated organic lemon zest

For the sauce:

2 onions
1 small carrot
3.5 oz (100 g) celeriac
1 tbsp oil
2 tsp icing sugar
1 tbsp tomato paste
1 cup (250 ml) strong red wine
5 cups (1.2 liters) poultry stock
1–2 tsp cornstarch
1 marjoram sprig
2 parsley sprigs
2 slices each of ginger and garlic
2 strips organic orange peel
0.7 oz (20 g) cold butter
salt

4 servings

1 Preheat the oven to 425 °F (220 °C). Cut the wings and neck off the goose and remove innards. Rinse the goose inside and out and pat dry. Chop goose wings and goose neck into 1.2 inch (3 cm) large pieces and place on a cookie sheet. Roast the pieces in the middle of the oven for 30 minutes until golden brown. Reserve for the sauce and remove drippings. Lower the oven temperature to 300 °F (150 °C). Place an oven rack in the bottom with a dripping pan underneath.

2 For the stuffing, cut the pretzel sticks into 0.4 inch (1 cm) cubes and put into a bowl. Bring the milk to a boil, remove from stove and blend with the eggs. Season the egg-milk mixture with salt, pepper and nutmeg. Pour over the pretzel dice and mix well. Peel and finely dice onions. Melt a tablespoon butter in a skillet and braise the diced onion over low heat until translucent. Combine with the pretzel-stick mixture. Blend the bratwurst sausage meat with the cream until smooth. Add together with parsley to the stuffing and mix. Season with lemon zest, salt, pepper and nutmeg.

3 Salt the cavity of the goose. Fill the cavity with the stuffing and close with a skewer. Roast the goose on the oven rack for 5 to 5 1/2 hours until crisp. Melt the remaining butter, season with salt and baste the goose at intervals.

4 For the sauce: Peel onions, carrot and celeriac and cut into about 0.4 inch (1 cm) cubes. Heat oil in a skillet and braise the vegetables. Caramelize the icing sugar in a saucepan over low heat. Stir in the tomato paste and brown lightly. Deglaze with half of the red wine and reduce to syrupy consistency. Add the remaining red wine and reduce again. Stir in the browned bones, the vegetables dice and the stock. Allow to simmer just below the boiling point for about 1 hour.

5 Strain the sauce through a fine sieve into a saucepan and reduce by half. Dissolve the starch in a bit of cold water and stir into the sauce. Simmer for 2 minutes. Add marjoram and parsley sprigs as well as ginger, garlic and orange peel, leave to infuse for a few minnutes and remove again. Stir the butter and some of the goose dripping (from the dripping pan) into the sauce and season with salt.

6 Carefully cut away the goose breasts and legs. Cut open the carcass with kitchen scissors, take out the stuffing and cut into slices. Arrange the legs, breasts and the stuffing with the sauce on warmed plates. The stuffed goose goes well with red cabbage (see page 145) or horseradish savoy cabbage (see page 150).

Pot Roasted Guinea Fowl Legs

2 onions · 1 carrot
5 oz (150 g) celeriac
4 Guinea fowl legs à about 7 oz (200 g) with skin, ready to cook
2–3 tbsp oil
1–2 tsp icing sugar
1 tbsp tomato paste
2 tbsp cognac
5 cl red port wine
7 fl oz (200 ml) strong red wine
2 1/2 cups (600 ml) poultry stock
1 bay leaf
5 juniper berries, slightly crushed
1/2 tsp black peppercorns
1 tbsp dried button mushrooms
1 garlic clove
1 strip organic orange peel
1 sliver of cinnamon bark
2 slices ginger
1 small thyme sprig
0.7 oz (20 g) cold butter
salt · freshly ground pepper

4 servings

1 Peel onions, carrot and the celeriac and cut into 0.4 to 0.6 inch (1 to 1 1/2 cm) cubes. Rinse the Guinea fowl legs, pat dry and remove thigh bone using a sharp knife.

2 Heat one or two tablespoons of oil in a wide casserole (or Dutch oven). Add legs and brown skin side down over medium heat. Turn over and sear the other side briefly. Remove Guinea fowl legs, and absorb remaining oil in the pan with paper towel.

3 Dust the icing sugar into the casserole and caramelize lightly. Stir in the tomato paste and brown lightly. Deglaze with cognac, port wine and half of the red wine and reduce to syrupy consistency. Add the remaining red wine and reduce again.

4 Preheat the oven to 325 °C (160 °C). Heat the remaining oil in a skillet and sauté the vegetable dice over medium heat lightly. Add vegetables to the reduced red wine in the casserole and pour in the broth. Carefully place the Guinea fowl legs skin side up on top of the mixture avoiding contact between the skin and the sauce.

5 Roast the legs in the middle of the oven without lid for 45 to 50 minutes until tender. After 30 minutes of cooking time, add bay leaf, juniper berries, peppercorns and the mushrooms and finish roasting. Remove cooked legs, place on a serving dish and keep warm.

6 Reduce the roasting liquid a bit more over low heat on top of the stove. Peel the garlic clove and cut in half. Add the garlic halves, the orange peel, the cinnamon sliver, ginger and thyme sprig and leave to infuse for a few minutes. Pass the sauce through a sieve, pressing the vegetables through well. Stir in butter and season with salt and pepper.

Alfons Schuhbeck

"Guinea fowl legs can be served with herb mashed potatoes or lemon mashed potatoes (both see page 156)."

Rabbit Saddle Fillets in Herb Oil

4 rabbit saddle fillets à about 3.5 oz (100 g), ready to cook
1 tbsp oil · 5 tbsp olive oil
1 strip each of organic lemon and orange peel
1 garlic clove, unpeeled
1 slice ginger · 1 bay leaf
1/4 scraped vanilla pod
1 sliver of cinnamon bark
ground cardamom
ground coriander
1/4 tsp allspice corns
2 small pieces of star anise
1 rosemary sprig
salt · freshly ground pepper

4 servings

1 Preheat the oven to 210 °F (100 °C). Place an oven rack in the middle with a dripping pan underneath. Rinse the rabbit saddle fillets and pat dry.

2 Heat the one tablespoon of oil in a skillet and fry the rabbit saddle fillets to sear on all sides over medium heat for 6 to 7 minutes. Remove meat from skillet and let it rest on the oven rack in the oven for 15 to 20 minutes.

3 Gently heat the olive oil in a clean skillet. Add lemon and orange peel, garlic, ginger, bay leaf, vanilla pod, cinnamon bark and a pinch each of cardamom and coriander as well as allspice corns, the pieces of star anise and the rosemary sprig.

4 To coat, turn the rabbit saddle fillets for 1 to 2 minutes in the spiced oil and season with salt and pepper. Cut the meat into slices, arrange on warmed plates and drizzle with some of the spiced oil.

Medium-done Hare Saddle

4 hare saddle fillets à 3.5 oz (100 g), ready to cook
1 tbsp oil
flavored butter of choice, e.g. thyme butter (see page 103)
salt · freshly ground pepper

4 servings

1 Preheat the oven to 210 °F 100 °C). Place an oven rack in the middle with a dripping pan underneath. Rinse the hare saddle and pat dry.

2 Heat the oil in a skillet and briefly sear the hare saddle from all sides over medium heat. Remove from skillet and allow to rest in the oven on the rack for 15 to 20 minutes until still pink inside.

3 Prepare the flavored butter in a pan and coat the hare saddle with mixture over low heat. Season with salt and pepper. Cut the meat into slices and arrange on warmed plates with the flavored butter.

Rabbit Legs in Red Wine Sauce

14 oz (400 g) shallots
2 carrots
2 ribs celery
2–3 tbsp oil
4 rabbit legs à 10–12 oz (300–350 g), ready to cook
1 tsp icing sugar
1 tbsp tomato paste
1/3 cup (70 ml) port wine
5/8 cup (150 ml) strong red wine
2 1/8 cups (500 ml) poultry stock
1 bay leaf
1 sliver of cinnamon bark
5 juniper berries
1 tsp black peppercorns
1/2 tsp allspice corns
1 tsp cornstarch
1 garlic clove
1 strip each of organic lemon and orange peel
2 thyme sprigs
0.3 oz (10 g) cold butter
salt · freshly ground pepper

4 servings

1 Peel shallots and cut in half. Clean carrots, peel and cut in half lengthwise. Cut diagonally into 1.6 to 2 inch (4 to 5 cm) long pieces. Clean celery, wash and cut diagonally into pieces similar in size. Heat one tablespoon of oil in a skillet and braise the vegetables for 2 to 3 minutes. Rinse the rabbit legs and pat dry.

2 Heat the remaining oil in a casserole (or Dutch oven), lightly sear the rabbit legs on all sides over low heat and remove from pan. Dust the icing sugar into the pan and caramelize lightly. Stir in the tomato paste and simmer briefly. Deglaze with the port wine and repeatedly deglaze and reduce with one third of the red wine each time.

3 Pour in the broth, add the vegetables and the rabbit legs and cover the pan with the lid, leaving open a small gap. Stew the meat until tender just below the boiling point for about 1 1/2 hours. In the meantime, fill bay leaf, cinnamon bark sliver, juniper berries, peppercorns and allspice corns in a small spice bag. Add the small spice bag after about 1 hour of the cooking time and allow the aromas to infuse the sauce.

4 Strain the sauce through a sieve into a saucepan, set aside vegetables and meat and remove spice bag. Reduce the sauce to half. Dissolve the cornstarch in a bit of cold water and stir into the sauce. Allow sauce to simmer over low heat for 2 minutes.

5 Peel garlic and cut in half. Add garlic halves, lemon and orange peel as well as the thyme sprigs to the sauce. Let everything sit for a few minutes and remove seasonings again. Stir in the butter and season the sauce with salt and pepper. Place the rabbit legs and the vegetables back into the sauce and warm up everything.

6 Arrange the rabbit legs with the vegetables and the sauce on warmed plates.

"I serve the rabbit legs with Topfen spaetzle (see page 161) or mixed vegetables (see page 148)."

Deer Shoulder with Roasted Pear

For the deer shoulder:

1 onion · 1 small carrot
4 oz (120 g) celeriac
2 tbsp oil
1 deer shoulder, about 3.1 lb (1.4 kg)
1–2 tsp icing sugar
1 tbsp tomato paste
1 1/4 cups (300 ml) strong red wine
1 1/4 cups (300 ml) poultry stock
1 bay leaf
5 juniper berries
1 tsp black peppercorns
1 tsp allspice corns
1 tsp cornstarch
1 garlic clove
1 thyme sprig
1 strip each of organic lemon and orange peel
2 tsp dried button mushrooms
1.4 oz (40 g) cold butter
salt · freshly ground pepper

For the pear:

1 small ripe, firm pear
1 tsp each of allspice corns and black peppercorns
0.7 oz (20 g) cold butter
1 bay leaf
1/4 scraped vanilla pod
1 tbsp pear brandy
juice of 1/2 orange

4 servings

1 For the deer shoulder: Peel onion, carrot and celeriac and cut into 0.4 inch (1 cm) cubes. Heat a tablespoon of oil in a skillet and braise the vegetable cubes for 2 to 3 minutes. Rinse the deer shoulder and pat dry. Remove excess fat, coarse tendons and bones. Tie the meat together with a kitchen twine.

2 Heat the remaining oil in a casserole (or Dutch oven), sear the meat lightly on all sides over medium heat and remove. Dust the icing sugar into the casserole and caramelize. Stir in the tomato paste and simmer briefly. Deglaze and reduce to syrupy consistency several times, using one third of the red wine every time. Pour the stock in the casserole, add vegetables and place the deer roast on top. Leave a small gap when covering with the lid. Cook the deer meat just below the boiling point for about 2 1/2 hours, turning the roast from time to time.

3 Remove roast from sauce and keep warm. Pass the sauce through a sieve into a saucepan, stirring and mashing down on the vegetables. Add bay leaf, juniper berries, peppercorns and allspice corns to the sauce and simmer to reduce a bit more. Dissolve the cornstarch in a bit of cold water, stir into the sauce and simmer for 2 minutes. Peel garlic and cut in half. Add garlic, thyme sprig, lemon and orange peel as well as the dried mushrooms to the sauce and leave to infuse for a few minutes. Pass everything through a sieve, stir in the butter and season the sauce with salt and pepper.

4 For the pear: Wash the pear, cut into quarters and core. Slice the quarters into thin wedges. Fill peppercorns and allspice corns into a spice grinder. Melt half of the butter in a skillet and fry the pear wedges briefly. Add bay leaf and vanilla pod. Pour in pear brandy and orange juice and simmer to reduce slightly. Add the remaining butter on top of the pear and melt. Season with freshly ground allspice and pepper (from the spice grinder). Season the deer sauce with cooking juices from the pear.

5 Cut the meat into slices, place it back into the sauce and warm up. Arrange the sliced meat with the sauce on warmed plates and garnish with the roasted pear wedges.

Pan-fried Deer Medallions

8 deer medallions à about 3 oz (80 g), from the saddle fillet
1 tbsp oil
flavored butter of choice, e.g. lemon-orange butter
salt · freshly ground pepper

4 servings

1 Preheat the oven to 210 °F (100 °C). Place an oven rack in the middle with a dripping pan underneath. Rinse the deer medallions and pat dry.

2 Press the medallions flat, using the palm of your hand. Heat the oil in a skillet and sear the medallions briefly on both sides over low heat. Remove meat from skillet and allow to finish cooking in the oven on the oven rack for about 30 minutes until still medium-done (inside pink).

3 Prepare the flavored butter in a skillet, coat the deer medallions with the butter over low heat and season with salt and pepper. Cut the meat into slices and arrange on warmed plates with the flavored butter.

Rack of Venison

1.3 lb (600 g) rack of venison or rack of wild boar, meat removed from the bone, ready to cook
1 tbsp oil
flavored butter of choice, e.g. thyme butter (see page 103)
salt · freshly ground pepper

4 servings

1 Preheat the oven to 210 °F (100 °C). Place an oven rack in the middle with a dripping pan underneath. Rinse the rack of venison and pat dry.

2 Heat the oil in a skillet and sear the rack of venison over medium heat briefly on all sides. Remove meat from skillet and allow to finish cooking in the oven on the oven rack for about 50 minutes until still pink inside.

3 Prepare the flavored butter in a skillet, coat the meat with the butter over low heat and season with salt and pepper. Cut the meat into slices and arrange on warmed plates with the flavored butter.

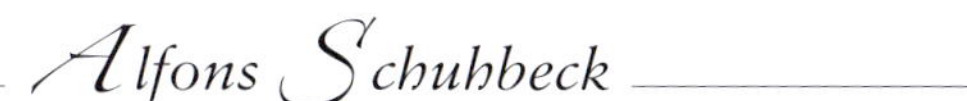

"I prepare rack of wild boar in the same fashion as the rack of venison. Deer or wild boar medallions (0.8 to 1.2 inches / 2 to 3 cm thick) are prepared like venison medallions (described above). However, they require 40 minutes cooking time until ready."

Medium-done Roast Saddle of Venison with Potato-Celery Puree

For the sauce:

3.3 lb (1.5 kg) saddle of venison, with bones
2 onions · 1 carrot
5 oz (150 g) celeriac
1 tbsp oil
1 tsp icing sugar
1 tbsp tomato paste
1 1/4 cups (300 ml) strong red wine
2 quarts (2 liters) poultry or vegetable stock (low salt)
2 tsp cornstarch
1/2 tsp allspice corns
1 bay leaf
1/2 tsp juniper berries, lightly crushed
1 sliver of cinnamon bark
1 strip each of organic lemon and orange peel
1/2 tsp grated dark chocolate
1/2 tbsp cranberry sauce
salt · freshly ground pepper
0.3 oz (10 g) cold butter

For the saddle of venison:

1 tbsp oil · 1 tbsp butter
1 tsp juniper berries
salt · freshly ground pepper

For the puree:

1.3 lb (600 g) celeriac · salt
10 oz (300 g) potatoes
caraway seeds
1/4 cup (60 ml) milk
1 tbsp butter
1 tbsp brown butter (see page 26)
cayenne pepper
freshly grated nutmeg

4 servings

1 For the sauce: Preheat the oven to 425 °F (220 °C). Rinse the venison saddle and pat dry. Release the fillets with a sharp boning knife from the bone. Remove all tendons and discard. Chop bones and rinse. Spread the bone pieces on a cookie sheet and brown lightly in the oven on middle rack for 30 minutes. Remove any grease. Peel onions, carrot and celeriac and cut into 0.8 inch (2 cm) cubes. Heat the oil in a skillet, add vegetables and braise lightly.

2 Caramelize the icing sugar in a large saucepan over medium heat. Add tomato paste and brown slightly. Deglaze repeatedly with thirds of the red wine and reduce every time to syrupy consistency. Add the browned bones and braised vegetables to the saucepan. Add stock and gently simmer the vegetables over low heat just below the boiling point for about 2 hours until cooked.

3 Strain the sauce through a sieve into a saucepan and simmer until reduced by half. Dissolve the cornstarch in a bit of cold water and stir until smooth. Add to the simmering sauce while stirring continually. Add allspice corns, bay leaf, juniper berries, cinnamon bark sliver, lemon and orange peel, leave to infuse for a few minutes and remove again. Season the sauce with dark chocolate, cranberry sauce, salt and pepper and stir in the butter at the end.

4 For the saddle of venison: Preheat the oven to 210 °F (100 °C). Place an oven rack in the middle of the oven with a dripping pan underneath. Heat the oil in a skillet and sear the venison fillets over medium heat on all sides. Remove meat from skillet and set on the oven rack to finish cooking for about 50 minutes until still pink inside. In the skillet, melt the butter over low heat and add juniper berries. Season with salt and pepper and turn the fillets to coat with the mixture.

5 For the puree: Peel celeriac, cut into 0.4 inch (1 cm) cubes and cook in salted water until soft for 15 to 20 minutes. Pour into a sieve to drain well. Purée the celeriac cubes with a wand mixer. Wash potatoes and cook in salted water with a pinch of caraway seeds for 15 to 20 minutes until soft. Pour into a sieve to drain. Peel as hot as possible and press through a fine sieve into a bowl. Mix with the celeriac puree. Warm up the milk and stir into puree with a silicone scraper. Add butter and brown butter and season the puree with salt and a pinch each of cayenne pepper and nutmeg.

6 Slice the venison fillet and arrange on warmed plates with sauce and potato-celery puree. Black salsify-brussel sprout vegetables are a good additional side dish.

Venison Ragout with Grapes and Bacon

For the ragout:

2.2 lb (1 kg) venison meat, from shoulder
2 onions · 1 carrot
5 oz (150 g) celeriac
2 tbsp oil
2 tsp icing sugar
1 tbsp tomato paste
2 fl oz (50 ml) cognac
1 1/4 cups (300 ml) strong red wine
3 1/8 cups (750 ml) poultry stock
1 bay leaf
1/2 tsp black peppercorns
5 juniper berries, lightly crushed
ground coriander
5 allspice corns
1 garlic clove
1 slice ginger
1 strip organic lemon peel
1 tsp icing sugar
5 tbsp red wine vinegar
1 tbsp currant jelly
salt · freshly ground pepper
0.3 oz (10 g) grated dark chocolate
1 oz (30 g) cold butter

Additional ingredients:

4 thin slices streaky bacon
1 tsp oil
3 oz (80 g) small seedless green grapes
1/2–1 tbsp butter

4 servings

1 For the ragout: Rinse the venison meat, pat dry and remove any thick tendons. Cut meat into 1.2 to 1.6 inch (3 to 4 cm) cubes. Peel onions, carrot and celeriac and cut into 0.4 inch (1 cm) cubes. Braise the vegetables in a skillet with 1 EL of oil over medium heat for 2 to 3 minutes.

2 Heat the remaining oil in a casserole (or Dutch oven). Sear the venison cubes over medium heat in two portions on all sides. Remove from pan. Dust one teaspoon of icing sugar into casserole and caramelize lightly. Stir in the tomato paste and brown. Deglaze with cognac and repeatedly deglaze with thirds of the red wine, reducing until creamy every time. Pour in stock, add venison meat and vegetables and stew over low heat just below the boiling point for 1 1/2 hours. After 1 hour of stewing, add bay leaf, peppercorns, juniper berries, a pinch of ground coriander and the allspice corns.

3 Strain sauce through a sieve into a saucepan and press through the vegetables. Set aside the meat cubes. Peel garlic and cut in half. Add garlic with ginger and orange peel to the sauce, leave to infuse over low heat for a few minutes and remove again. Lightly caramelize the remaining teaspoon of icing sugar in a skillet, deglaze with vinegar and reduce by half. Season the stewing sauce with currant jelly, salt, pepper and reduced vinegar. Melt the chocolate in the sauce and stir in the butter in small pieces. Return the meat to the sauce and warm up.

4 Prepare for serving by cutting bacon slices into 0.4 to 0.8 inch (1 to 2 cm) large strips. Heat the oil in a skillet and fry the bacon strips over medium heat until crisp. Remove and drain on paper towel. Wash the grapes, drain, possibly remove skin and cut in half, depending on the size. Melt the butter in a skillet and braise the grapes over low heat for 1 to 2 minutes. Serve the venison ragout on warmed plates and garnish with bacon strips and grapes. Serve with spaetzle (see page 161), potato puree (see page 156) or pretzel dumplings (see page 153).

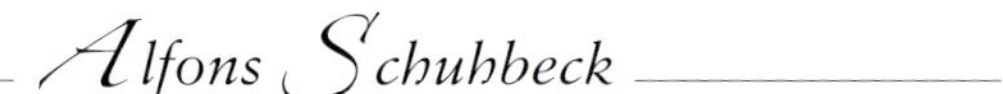

"Deer stew can be prepared the same way. Substitute the venison meat with deer meat from shoulder or haunch. For hare ragout, I use hind and forelegs."

Wild Boar Roast

3 onions · 1 carrot
5 oz (150 g) celeriac
3 tbsp oil
3.3 lb (1.5 kg) wild boar shoulder
1–2 tsp icing sugar
1 tbsp tomato paste
1 1/4 cups (300 ml) strong red wine
3 1/8 cups (750 ml) poultry stock
1 tsp juniper berries
1/2 tsp allspice corns
1 tsp black peppercorns
1 tsp fennel seeds
1 bay leaf
2 tbsp dried button mushrooms
1 tsp cornstarch
1 strip organic orange peel
1 slice ginger
1/2 garlic clove, peeled
1 rosemary sprig
1/2 tsp grated dark chocolate
0.7 oz (20 g) cold butter
salt · freshly ground pepper

4 servings

1 Preheat the oven to 300 °F (150 °C). Peel onions, carrot and celeriac and cut into 0.4 to 0.6 inch (1 to 1 1/2 cm) large pieces. Heat a tablespoon of oil in a skillet and braise the vegetables for 2 to 3 minutes. Rinse the boar shoulder and pat dry. Remove large tendons.

2 Heat the remaining oil in a roasting pan, briefly sear the boar shoulder on all sides over medium heat and remove. Dust the icing sugar into the roasting pan and caramelize lightly. Stir in the tomato paste and braise briefly. Deglaze repeatedly with thirds of the red wine and reduce every time until creamy. Pour in the stock, add vegetables and boar roast.

3 Stew the boar roast covered in the oven on the middle rack for 2 1/2 hours until tender. Remove meat from roasting pan and keep warm.

4 Add juniper berries, allspice corns, peppercorns, fennel seeds, bay leaf and dried mushrooms to the sauce and simmer a bit more to reduce on top of the stove. Strain the sauce through a sieve into a saucepan, pressing lightly on the vegetables.

5 Dissolve the cornstarch in a bit of cold water and stir until smooth. Mix into the sauce and simmer for 2 minutes. Add orange peel, ginger, garlic and the rosemary sprig, leave to infuse for a few minutes and remove again. Melt chocolate in the sauce and stir in the butter. Season with salt and pepper.

6 Cut the roast into slices and arrange on warmed plates with sauce. Serve with potato puree (see page 156), spaetzle (see page 161) or pretzel dumplings (see page 153).

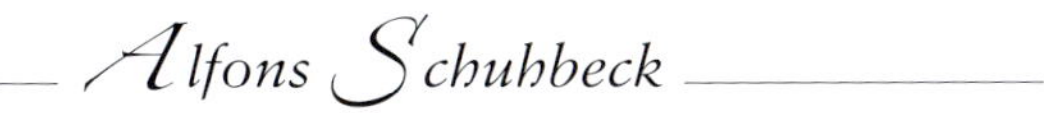

"Shoat haunch can be cooked just like boar shoulder."

Vegetables & Side Dishes

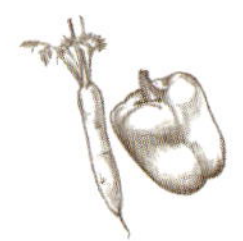

Sauerkraut Variations

1 large onion
1 tbsp oil
1.7 lb (800 g) canned sauerkraut
3.5 oz (100 ml) dry white wine
1 2/3 cups (400 ml) vegetable stock
1 piece bacon rind or 1 thick piece streaky bacon
5 black peppercorns
2 juniper berries, slightly crushed
1 bay leaf
2 tbsp apple sauce
1 tbsp butter
cayenne pepper · sugar

4 servings

1 Peel and finely dice onion. Heat the oil in a skillet and braise the onion cubes over low heat until translucent. Add sauerkraut and steam briefly. Add white wine and reduce completely.

2 Pour in the vegetable stock and add bacon. Stew the sauerkraut over low heat for about 45 minutes. In the meantime, fill a small spice bag with peppercorns, juniper berries and bay leaf and close bag. After 30 minutes of cooking time, add apple sauce and spice bag to sauerkraut.

3 Remove spice bag when finished cooking. Stir in the butter and season the sauerkraut with a pinch each of cayenne pepper and sugar.

For creamed sauerkraut: Prepare as above. At the end of cooking time, stir in 2 fl oz (50 g) cream and three tablespoons butter.

For pepper sauerkraut: Prepare the sauerkraut as above. At the end of cooking time, add 2 fl oz (50 g) cream, three tablespoons butter and a lot of cayenne pepper and mix. In Bavaria, pepper sauerkraut is often served with regional specialties like liver dumplings (see page 43), Surbraten (made from cured pork) or Rinderbackerl (beef cheeks).

For champagne sauerkraut: Substitute white wine with champagne. Champagne sauerkraut is excellent served with roasted pheasant breast.

For coconut-curry sauerkraut: Prepare the sauerkraut as above, but add 1 cup (250 ml) broth and 5/8 cup (150 ml) coconut milk (canned). At the end of cooking time, add one or two teaspoons mild curry powder. Coconut-curry sauerkraut goes well with rostbratwurst, roasted chicken or turkey breast.

Alfons Schuhbeck

"I only add the apple sauce when the sauerkraut is done, to avoid sauerkraut sticking a lot to the bottom of the pan. Apple sauce adds a fruity note to the sauerkraut and thickens it a little bit."

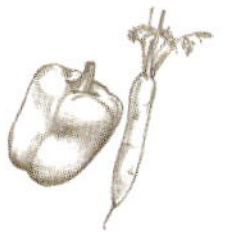

Red Cabbage Variations

1.7 lb (800 g) red cabbage
1 tbsp icing sugar
3.4 fl oz (100 ml) port wine
7 fl oz (200 ml) strong red wine
1/2 cup (125 ml) vegetable stock
1 bay leaf
5 allspice corns
1/2 tsp black peppercorns
1 sliver of cinnamon bark
2–3 tbsp apple sauce
1 strip organic orange peel
1 slice ginger
0.7 oz (20 g) cold butter
salt · sugar
1 tbsp mild balsamic vinegar

4 servings

1 Clean red cabbage, remove outer leaves and cut out the stalk. Cut the cabbage leaves into fine strips with a vegetable slicer. Caramelize the icing sugar in a saucepan, deglaze with port wine and red wine and reduce to about one third. Add red cabbage and stock. Gently simmer for about 1 1/2 hours over low heat with lid closed, stirring often.

2 Add bay leaf after 1 hour of cooking time. Fill a small spice bag with allspice corns, peppercorns and cinnamon bark sliver. Close the bag and add to red cabbage.

3 Stir apple sauce into red cabbage when done. Add orange peel and ginger, leave to infuse for a few minutes and remove again. Remove bay leaf and spice bag and stir in the butter. Season the red cabbage with salt, sugar and vinegar.

For chocolate flavored red cabbage: Prepare cabbage as above described. At the end of cooking time, stir in a half or one teaspoon chopped dark chocolate shavings.

For elderberry-pear red cabbage: Prepare as outlined in steps 1 and 2. Peel a pear, cut into quarters and core. Cut quarters into small wedges. Add pear wedges with 2 fl oz (50 ml) elderberry juice to red cabbage about 10 minutes before the end of cooking time. If you happen to have elderberry-pear compote, mix 5 oz (150 g) into cabbage when finished cooking. You can also add cut plums into the elderberry-pear red cabbage if you like.

"All red cabbage variations go well with game, duck, goose and dark stewed casseroles."

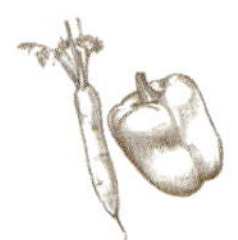

Bavarian Cabbage with Quince

1/2 small head of white cabbage
1/2 quince
1 small carrot
1 onion
1 garlic clove
1 tbsp oil
a dash of apple juice
7 fl oz (200 ml) vegetable stock
salt · cayenne pepper
ground caraway seeds
1 tbsp freshly chopped parsley leaves
1 tbsp butter
a dash of apple vinegar

4 servings

1 Clean white cabbage, remove outer leaves and cut out the stalk. Peel the quince, cut into quarters and core. Cut the white cabbage and quince into diamond shapes. Clean carrots and dice finely.

2 Peel onion and garlic and cut into small cubes. Heat the oil in a skillet and braise onion and garlic dice over medium heat until translucent. Add cabbage and quince pieces and stew briefly. Add diced carrot and deglaze with a dash of apple juice.

3 Pour in the stock. Stew the vegetables for 20 to 30 minutes until tender with the lid closed.

4 Season the Bavarian cabbage with salt and a pinch each of cayenne pepper and ground caraway seeds. Stir in parsley and butter. Season with a dash of apple vinegar.

For Bavarian cabbage with bacon: Cut 3.5 oz (100 g) streaky bacon into small cubes and fry in a skillet over medium heat in a tablespoon of oil. Remove bacon cubes and drain on paper towel. Mix with the cooked cabbage.

"Traditionally, white (green) cabbage is cut into strips or sliced for Bavarian cabbage, steamed with onions in broth, and seasoned with a dash of vinegar, a bit of salt, sugar and ground caraway seeds. According to taste, a pear can be substituted for the quince. Because pears are softer, pear cubes should be added after 15 or 20 minutes of cooking time."

Mixed Vegetables

4 oz (120 g) baby carrots with greens
salt · 4 oz (120 g) g sugar snaps (mangetout)
7 oz (200 g) romanesco broccoli or as an alternative: broccoli
1/3 cup (80 ml) vegetable stock
1 tbsp butter · 1 red chili pepper
freshly ground pepper
freshly grated nutmeg
1/2 tsp grated organic lime zest
1 tbsp lime juice
1 tbsp mild olive oil

4 servings

1 Cut off the greens from the carrots leaving 0.4 inch (1 cm). Wash the carrots, but do not cut, and cook them in salted water until firm to the bite. Strain, refresh with cold water and peel.

2 Wash the sugar snaps, cut off the ends and cut the pods in half. Divide romanesco broccoli into small flowerets. Peel the stalk and cut into slices. One after another, blanch sugar snaps and the flowerets and slices of romanesco broccoli in salted water until firm to the bite. Remove with a skimmer, refresh with cold water and drain.

3 Heat up all of the different types of vegetables with the stock in a large saucepan. Stir in the butter. Add chili pepper and leave to infuse for 3 minutes. Season the vegetables with salt, pepper, nutmeg, lime peel, lime juice and olive oil. Remove chili pepper.

Cauliflower with Buttered Bread Crumbs

4 tbsp white bread crumbs
4 tbsp butter
salt · freshly ground pepper
1.5 lb (700 g) cauliflower
1/4 cup (60 ml) vegetable stock
4 tbsp butter
cayenne pepper
freshly grated nutmeg

4 servings

1 For the bread crumbs, roast white bread crumbs in a pan with butter over medium heat until golden brown. Season with salt and pepper.

2 For the vegetables, wash the cauliflower and divide into small flowerets. Cook firm to the bite in salted water for 6 to 8 minutes. Pour into a sieve, refresh with cold water and drain.

3 Heat up the cauliflower flowerets in a deep pan with the stock. Add butter and season the cauliflower with salt and a pinch each of cayenne pepper and nutmeg. To serve, spoon the buttered bread crumbs over cauliflower.

Alfons Schuhbeck

"Flavor can be rounded off by adding a tablespoon of freshly chopped parsley leaves to the cauliflower. Alternatively, serve with orange crumbs: Mix 1/2 teaspoon of grated organic orange zest into the roasted crumbs."

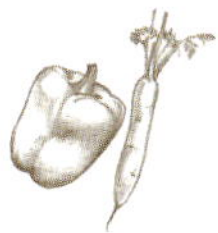

Paprika Casserole

2 red bell peppers
1 yellow bell pepper
1 onion
1 small zucchini, about 7 oz (200 g)
3 tbsp olive oil
1 bay leaf
3.4 fl oz (100 ml) vegetable stock
1 garlic clove
3.5 oz (100 g) strained tomatoes (canned)
1 thyme sprig
1 sliver of cinnamon bark
1/4 scraped vanilla pod
salt · freshly ground pepper
cayenne pepper

4 servings

1 Cut the red and yellow bell peppers lengthwise in half, core and rinse. Cut the peppers into 0.6 inch (1 1/2 cm) pieces. Peel onion and cut into pieces of the same size. Clean zucchini, wash, cut lengthwise in half and then into 0.2 inch (5 mm) wide slices.

2 Heat a tablespoon olive oil in a saucepan and braise the bell pepper and onion pieces over medium heat until onions are translucent. Add bay leaf. Pour in the stock and stew the vegetables over low heat for about 8 minutes with the lid closed. Peel garlic and cut in half.

3 Add zucchini slices, strained tomatoes, garlic, thyme sprig as well as cinnamon bark sliver and vanilla pod. Stew peppers for another 2 to 3 minutes. Stir in the remaining olive oil and season with salt, pepper and a pinch of cayenne pepper. Remove bay leaf, garlic, thyme sprig, cinnamon bark and vanilla pod.

Pickled Pumpkin

1.3 lb (600 g) 'Muscade de provence' pumpkin or butternut squash e.g. Waltham Butternut
5 oz (150 g) sugar
7 fl oz (200 ml) white wine vinegar
1 tsp salt · 2 slices ginger · 2 cloves
1 bay leaf · 2 juniper berries
1 tsp mustard corns
1/2 tsp black peppercorns

4 servings

1 Peel pumpkin, core and cut into 0.6 to 0.8 inch (1 1/2 to 2 cm) cubes – yields about 14 oz (400 g) pumpkin cubes.

2 Caramelize the sugar lightly in a saucepan over medium heat. Add pumpkin cubes, 1 2/3 cups (400 ml) water as well as vinegar, salt and spices. Cook all ingredients for 1 minute over medium heat. Transfer the pumpkin with liquid and spices evenly into two large canning jars or jars with twist-off lids. Close the jars immediately and allow the pumpkin cubes to cool down. The pickled pumpkin cubes can be stored for several months in the refrigerator.

"Pickled pumpkins are great with smoked meat, but can also be mixed into potato salad. Alternatively, serve them with lamb's lettuce and fried liver or roasted duck (see page 128)."

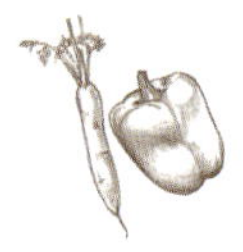

Creamed Savoy Cabbage

1 head of savoy cabbage
salt
7 fl oz (200 g) cream
1 oz (30 g) cold butter
cayenne pepper
freshly grated nutmeg

4 servings

1 Clean savoy cabbage, take off the single leaves, cut in half and remove veins. Wash the leaves and blanch in salted water for several minutes until firm to the bite. Pour into a sieve, refresh with cold water and drain. Press excess water out of the leaves with hands. Cut the leaves into diamond shapes.

2 Heat up the savoy cabbage with cream in a pan. Stir in the butter and season with salt and a pinch each of cayenne pepper and nutmeg. According to taste, sprinkle with roughly chopped walnuts.

For horseradish-savoy: Prepare the savoy cabbage as above described and stir in one to three tablespoons of creamed horseradish (from a jar) according to taste.

Kale and Savoy Cabbage with Horseradish

1.1 lb (500 g) kale
1.1 lb (500 g) savoy cabbage
salt
1/3 cup (80 ml) vegetable stock
1/2 cup (120 g) cream
1 tbsp creamed horseradish (from a jar)
cayenne pepper
freshly grated nutmeg
a pinch of grated organic orange zest

4 servings

1 Pluck off the kale leaves from hard stems and cut the leaves into small pieces. Clean the savoy, separate in single leaves and remove veins. Wash both sorts of cabbage.

2 Blanch kale pieces in salted water for about 4 minutes until firm to the bite. Pour into a sieve, refresh with cold water and drain. Cook the savoy leaves in salted water for about 10 minutes. Pour into a sieve, refresh with cold water and drain. Squeeze excess water from both vegetables. Cut the savoy leaves into about 0.8 inch (2 cm) pieces.

3 In a saucepan, heat up kale and savoy with stock and cream. Stir in the creamed horseradish and season the cabbage-horseradish mixture with salt, some cayenne pepper as well as nutmeg and orange zest.

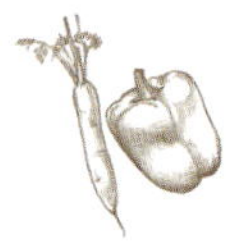

Cooked Potato Dumplings

For the filling:

2 slices white bread
1–2 tbsp butter
1 tsp freshly chopped parsley leaves

For the dumplings:

2.6 lb (1.2 kg) potatoes
salt
1 tsp caraway seeds
3.5 oz (100 g) cornstarch
2 egg yolks
3 tbsp brown butter (see page 26)
freshly grated nutmeg

For 8 dumplings

1 For the filling: Cut the white bread into small cubes. Roast the bread cubes in a pan with butter over low heat until golden brown. Drain on paper towel and mix with parsley.

2 For the dumplings: Wash potatoes and cook with caraway seeds in abundant salted water. Pour off the water. Peel potatoes while hot and mash with a potato masher.

3 Weigh 2.2 lb (1 kg) from the mashed potatoes and add cornstarch, egg yolks, brown butter, salt and a pinch of nutmeg. Mix well until the dough is smooth.

4 With wet hands, form eight dumplings, press them somewhat flat, and fill them with bread cubes. Shape to smooth round dumplings. Simmer the dumplings in a saucepan of simmering water for about 20 minutes until done. Remove with a skimmer.

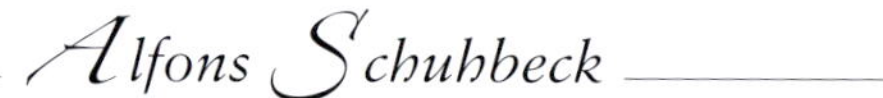

"The dumplings become more substantial if you add a few ham or bacon cubes to the filling. If you prepare the potato dumplings without filling, sprinkle them with some buttered crumbs. For the buttered crumbs, melt 3.5 oz (100 g) butter, add 2 oz (50 g) white bread crumbs and roast until golden brown."

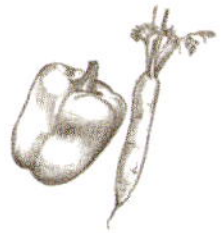

Bread Dumplings

10 oz (300 g) rolls or white bread, from the day before
2/3 cup (170 ml) milk
3 eggs
salt
freshly ground pepper
freshly grated nutmeg
1 tbsp freshly chopped parsley leaves

For 8 dumplings

1 For the bread dumplings (in Bavaria called Semmelknödel), cut the rolls or white bread into very thin slices. Boil the milk and remove from stove. Whisk eggs, stir into milk and season with salt, pepper and a pinch of nutmeg. Pour the egg-milk mixture over the bread slices and let everything sit for a several minutes with the lid closed.

2 Fold parsley into the softened bread slices. With wet hands, form eight dumplings from the mixture. Boil water in a large saucepan and let the dumplings sit in simmering water about 15 to 20 minutes.

For bacon dumplings: Mix rendered bacon cubes (pour off fried fat) and lightly braised onion dice into dumpling dough.

For herbal dumplings: Add three to five tablespoons of freshly chopped herbs.

Pretzel Dumplings

9 oz (250 g) soft pretzel sticks (sticks made of pretzel dough), from the day before
1 cup (250 ml) milk
2 eggs
salt
freshly ground pepper
freshly grated nutmeg
1/2 onion
1 tbsp oil
1 tbsp freshly chopped parsley leaves

8 servings

1 For the pretzel dumplings (in Bavaria called Brezenknödel), remove the salt from pretzel sticks. Cut the sticks into 0.2 to 0.4 inch (5 to 10 mm) cubes. Boil milk and remove from stove. Whisk eggs and stir in the milk a little bit at a time. Season the egg-milk mixture with salt, pepper and a pinch of nutmeg. Carefully fold in the pretzel stick dice, without mashing them.

2 Peel and finely dice onion. Heat the oil in a pan and braise the onion cubes until translucent. Fold onions and parsley into dumpling dough.

3 Spread out two sheets of kitchen foil next to each other on the work surface and place plastic wrap on each sheet. With wet hands, put equal amounts of dumpling dough on the foil and shape them into long rolls with a diameter of about 2 inches (5 cm). First wrap the rolls in plastic wrap and then in the kitchen foil. Press down on the ends of the kitchen foil, and turn around so that it becomes a tight uniform roll.

4 Gently simmer the dumpling rolls in a large saucepan with simmering water for about 30 minutes. Remove rolls with a skimmer and unwrap foil. Cut the rolls into slices while still hot.

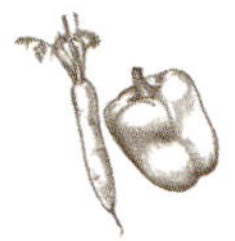

Bohemian Napkin Dumplings

5 slices white bread
3 oz (80 g) butter
9 oz (250 g) flour
salt · sugar
freshly grated nutmeg
0.7 oz (20 g) yeast
3/4 cup (175 ml) lukewarm milk
1 egg
1 egg yolk
melted butter for brushing
flour for shaping

8 servings

1 Cut the white bread into small cubes. Roast the white bread cubes with butter in a pan over medium heat until golden brown and drain on paper towel.

2 In a bowl, mix flour with half a teaspoon of salt, a pinch of sugar and some nutmeg. Crumble yeast with fingers and dissolve in lukewarm milk. Stir the yeast mixture with egg and egg yolk into flour and knead all ingredients with the dough hooks of an electric mixer until smooth. Mix in the roasted bread cubes. Cover the dough and leave to rise in a warm place for about 20 minutes.

3 Dampen three cloth napkins with water and brush well with butter. Shape the dough with the aid of some flour into three about 4 inch (10 cm) long rolls. Place each roll of dough on a napkin and turn the ends of the napkins over loosely. Leave to rise for another 25 minutes.

4 Bring abundant water to a boil in a flat, long saucepan. Wrap the rolls of dough in the napkins, but not too tight, in order that the dumplings are able to rise a little bit while cooking. Loosely tie the end of the kitchen twine. Place the napkin dumplings in the saucepan and cook them in lightly simmering water for about 35 minutes, turning occasionally.

5 Remove the dumpling rolls with a skimmer and drain. Roll the dumplings out of the napkins and cut into slices with a sharp knife.

"This dumpling is perfect for dishes with gravy because it soaks up sauce very well. Traditionally, the dumpling is cut into slices using a thread. Loop thread around dumpling crossing over and pull ends together."

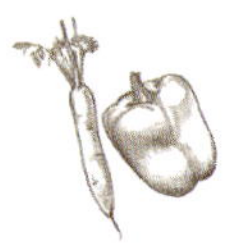

Potato Puree Variations

2.2 lb (1 kg) high starch potatoes
salt
1/2 tsp caraway seeds
1 cup (250) ml milk
1 tbsp butter
2 tbsp brown butter (see page 26)
freshly grated nutmeg

4 servings

1 Wash potatoes and boil in abundant salted water with caraway seeds until soft. Pour into a sieve, peel as hot as possible, and press through a potato press (or food mill).

2 Warm up the milk and mix well with the pressed through potatoes using a wooden spoon. Mix in butter and brown butter. Season the puree with salt and nutmeg.

For potato-lemon puree: Stir the grated zest of an organic lemon into prepared puree.

For potato-spinach puree: Pick through 3.5 oz (100 g) of young spinach, wash and drain. Remove coarse stems. Stir the spinach into prepared puree.

For potato-apple puree: Peel one apple, cut into quarters, core and dice finely. Stir the apple dice and two tablespoons of apple sauce into prepared puree.

For potato-pear puree: Peel, core and quarter two firm pears and cut into small cubes. Stir the pear cubes into prepared puree.

For potato puree with root vegetables: Purée 1.1 lb (500 g) of boiled root vegetables and stir into prepared puree.

For potato-leek puree: Purée 14 oz (400 g) of cooked leeks and stir into prepared puree.

For potato puree with bear's garlic: Wash 2 oz (50 g) of bear's garlic leaves, shake dry and cut into strips. Stir the bear's garlic strips into prepared puree.

For potato puree with mustard corns: Cook two tablespoons of mustard corns in salted water until tender. Drain in a sieve and rinse with cold water. Cut 3.5 oz (100 g) of breakfast bacon into small cubes, fry crispy in one or two tablespoons oil and drain on paper towel. Wash two endive leaves, shake dry and cut into fine strips. Stir mustard corns, bacon cubes and endive strips into prepared puree.

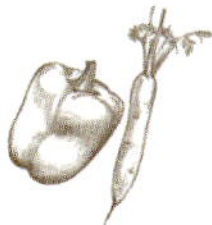

Reiberdatschi

1.1 lb (500 g) low starch potatoes
2 egg yolks
salt
freshly ground pepper
freshly grated nutmeg
2 tbsp oil

For 8 to 10 pieces

1 Wash the potatoes, peel and grate into fine strips on a vegetable grater. Squeeze the potato strips well with hands to drain. Mix egg yolks and potatoes. Season the mixture with salt, pepper and nutmeg.

2 Heat some oil in a skillet. Using a spoon, place some of the potato mixture into skillet and press flat to little pancakes with a diameter of 2.4 to 2.8 inches (6 to 7 cm). Fry the bottom of the pancakes for about 2 minutes until golden brown, turn and fry the other side for about 2 minutes as well. Remove Reiberdatschi from skillet and drain on paper towel. Continue to make potato pancakes until the batter is finished.

For Reiberdatschi with bacon and pears: Cut 3.5 oz (100 g) of bacon into very small cubes. Fry the cubes crispy in a skillet with one or two tablespoons of oil over low heat and drain on paper towel. Peel, core and quarter one pear and cut into very small cubes. Mix pear and bacon dice with the Reiberdatschi mixture and fry the pancakes as described above.

For Reiberdatschi with leeks: Cut 3.5 oz (100 g) of leeks (preferably the light green parts) into small cubes and mix with the Reiberdatschi mixture. Fry pancakes as described above.

"Reiberdatschi – in Bavarian dialect the name for potato pancakes – served with apple sauce or chive sauce are a separate dish, but they are also excellent as a side dish with matjes fillets.
For fruity Reiberdatschi, cut one peeled pear into small cubes and mix with the grated potatoes. Instead of pear, you can also use apple or quince."

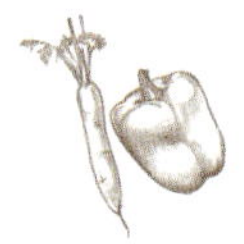

Potato Gratin

1 tbsp butter for the dish
1 2/3 cups (400 g) cream
1 garlic clove, peeled and halved
2 slices ginger
1 strip organic lemon peel
1 thyme sprig
salt
freshly ground pepper
freshly grated nutmeg
2.2 lb (1 kg) high starch potatoes

4 servings

1 Preheat the oven to 350 °F (180 °C). Grease an ovenproof dish with butter. In a saucepan, bring the cream to a boil and remove from stove. Add garlic, ginger, lemon peel and thyme sprig to the cream, leave to infuse for 5 minutes and remove again. Season the cream with salt, pepper and nutmeg.

2 Peel potatoes, wash and grate into very thin slices, less then 0.1 inch (2 mm). Mix the potato slices with cream, fill into dish and bake in the oven on the middle rack for about 40 minutes until golden brown. According to taste, sprinkle gratin with 3.5 oz (100 g) Alpine cheese before baking. For an even heartier flavor, season with a pinch of oregano.

Boiled Potatoes

1/2 onion
1 small bay leaf
2 cloves
2.2 lb (1 kg) low starch potatoes
salt
1 tsp black peppercorns

4 servings

Peel onion and fasten bay leaf with cloves on top. Wash potatoes and peel. Cook the potatoes in abundant salted water with peppercorns and spiked onion until soft. Drain the potatoes and serve as side dish with fish or meat entrees.

For garlic-chili potatoes: Replace peppercorns and spiked onion by adding half of a peeled garlic clove, one slice ginger and one small dried chili pepper to the salted water.

For coriander-cardamom potatoes: Add half of a peeled garlic clove, seven green cardamom pods, a tablespoon coriander corns and half teaspoon turmeric powder to the salted water instead of spiked onion and peppercorns.

Alfons Schuhbeck

"According to taste, boiled potatoes can be tossed in two or three tablespoons butter, brown butter (see page 26) or mild olive oil. For extra flavor, boil potatoes in vegetable or poultry stock."

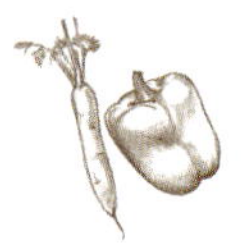

Finger Noodles

1.3 lb (600 g) high starch potatoes
salt
1 tsp caraway seeds
2 tbsp brown butter (see page 26)
2 egg yolks
2 oz (60 g) all purpose flour (ideally Wiener Griessler)
2 oz (60 g) cornstarch
freshly grated nutmeg
flour for work surface
1–2 tbsp oil
freshly ground pepper
2 tbsp butter

4 servings

1 Wash potatoes and cook in abundant salted water with caraway seeds until soft. Drain the potatoes, peel as hot as possible, and press through a potato press (or food mill). Leave to cool down for about 30 minutes.

2 Weigh 1.1 lb (500 g) of pressed through potatoes and mix with brown butter and egg yolks. Mix flour with cornstarch and sift on top of potato mixture. Knead until just blended. Season the finger-noodle dough with salt and nutmeg.

3 Divide the dough into three portions and shape each portion on a lightly floured work surface to ropes of about 0.6 inch (1 1/2 cm) diameter. Cut ropes into 1.2 inch (3 cm) long pieces and shape these with lightly floured hands into about 2.8 inch (7 cm) long ropes with pointed ends.

4 In a large saucepan, bring a sufficient quantity of salted water to the boiling point. Add finger noodles and gently simmer for a few minutes until they rise to the surface. Bring the finger noodles to a boil briefly once more and remove with a skimmer. Drain on paper towel.

5 Heat the oil in a skillet and fry the finger noodles over medium heat on all sides until golden brown. Season with salt and pepper, add butter and turn the finger noodles to coat.

"Once prepared, the finger noodle dough should be used right away to avoid changes in texture. This ensures that dough can be shaped well into noodles. For preparation of finger noodles in advance, spread out cooked noodles on a cookie sheet. Mix with one or two tablespoons of oil and leave to cool down. Finger noodles can be stored refrigerated in a container with tight fitting lid for one to two days. Fry just before serving as described above.
Gnocchi can be prepared with the same dough. In this case, cut ropes into 0.4 to 0.6 inch (1 to 1 1/2 cm) large pieces, cook in salted water, but do not fry."

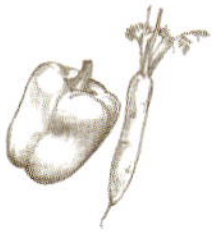

Spaetzle

14 oz (400 g) all purpose flour (ideally Wiener Griessler)
8 eggs
salt
1 tbsp oil
1–2 tbsp butter
freshly ground pepper
freshly grated nutmeg

4 servings

1 Combine flour with eggs, a tablespoon salt and the oil. Blend in the kitchen machine or with the dough hooks of an electric blender. Blend the dough another 3 to 5 minutes until bubbles form.

2 In a large saucepan, bring abundant salted water to a boil. Briefly dip the spaetzle grater in the water, fill with dough and grate the spaetzle into the boiling water.

3 Once spaetzle have risen to the surface, bring to a boil briefly once more. Remove with skimmer and toss to coat with melted butter in a skillet over medium heat. Season the spaetzle with salt, pepper and nutmeg.

Topfen Spaetzle

9 oz (250 g) all purpose flour (ideally Wiener Griessler)
2 oz (50 g) semolina
9 oz (250 g) farmer's cheese
5 eggs
salt
1/3 cup (80 ml) vegetable stock
1–2 tbsp butter
freshly ground pepper
freshly grated nutmeg

4 servings

1 Combine flour with semolina, farmer's cheese, eggs and some salt. Blend in the kitchen machine or with the dough hooks of an electric blender. Blend another 3 to 5 minutes until dough forms bubbles.

2 In a large saucepan, bring abundant salted water to a boil. Briefly dip the spaetzle grater in the water, fill with dough and grate the spaetzle into the boiling water.

3 Once spaetzle have risen to the surface, bring to a boil briefly once more. Remove with a skimmer. In a skillet, heat up the stock and add butter to melt. Briefly toss the spaetzle over middle heat in stock and butter to coat. Season with salt, pepper and nutmeg.

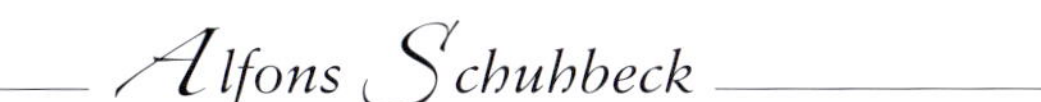

"For Topfen-Poppy Spaetzle cook two tablespoons of poppy seeds for 10 minutes in water. Drain in a sieve and stir into the dough. Cook as described above. Topfen is a special sort of quark or farmer's cheese."

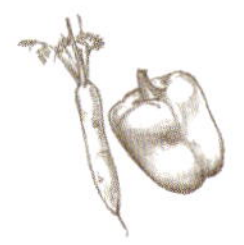

Rösti Variations

1.1 lb (500 g) low starch potatoes
salt
freshly ground pepper
freshly grated nutmeg
1–2 tbsp oil

4 servings

1 Wash potatoes, peel and grate on vegetable grater into fine strips. Season the potato strips with some salt, pepper and nutmeg and leave to infuse for a few minutes. To drain, squeeze well with hands.

2 Heat the oil in a skillet. Spread out potato strips in an even layer 0.2 inch (5 mm) thick and press down lightly. Fry the Rösti over medium heat for about 4 minutes until golden brown. To overturn, slide the Rösti from the skillet onto a plate, place the turned over skillet on top, flip and return Rösti to skillet. Add some oil and fry the other side until golden brown as well. Remove Rösti and drain on paper towel.

For vegetable Rösti: Choose 3.5 oz (100 g) leeks, 1 small carrot, 3.5 oz (100 g) fennel, 3.5 oz (100 g) celeriac or 3.5 oz (100 g) zucchini. Wash the vegetables and grate into fine strips. Mix vegetable strips and potato strips. Season and fry as described above.

For pear or apple Rösti. Peel, quarter and core one pear or one apple and cut or grate into fine strips. Mix strips with potato strips. Season and fry as described above.

For sauerkraut Rösti: Mix 3.5 oz (100 g) raw sauerkraut with the potato strips. Season and fry as described above.

For Rösti from cooked potatoes: Wash 10 oz (300 g) low starch potatoes and cook in abundant salted water with a pinch of caraway seeds for about 15 minutes. Drain and refresh with cold water. Peel potatoes and grate while still hot on a vegetable grater in coarse strips. Season with salt, pepper and nutmeg. Fry the Rösti in a skillet in three tablespoons of oil on both sides crispy brown.

"Who like it, can also choose to fry small Rösti: Simply place small heaps of potato strips into the skillet and flatten with spoon. Once grated, potatoes should be used right away so they do not lose their nice yellow color and do not become brown."

A. Schuhbeck

Pastries & Desserts

Strudel Dough (Basic Recipe)

10.5 oz (300 g) flour
salt
4 tbsp oil
1 egg yolk
flour for the work surface

For about 12 oz (350 g)

1 Sift flour into a bowl and sprinkle with a pinch of salt. Make a well in the center. Put three tablespoons of oil with 5/8 cup (150 ml) lukewarm water and the egg yolk into the well. Knead all of the ingredients either with an electric mixer with dough hooks, or empty ingredients onto a flour board and knead with your hands until the dough is smooth.

2 Cut the strudel dough in half, shape into two balls and brush the balls with the remaining oil. Wrap the balls of dough in plastic wrap and let them sit at room temperature for about 1 hour.

"Strudel dough should not be kneaded after it has been stirred, because it will get too tough to be pulled out thinly. Wrapped tightly it can be kept frozen in the freezer and taken out as needed. Let the dough thaw out slowly in the refrigerator."

Apple Strudel

For the filling:

8 apples, about 3.1 lb (1.4 kg)
2.5 oz (70 g) flaked almonds
2 oz (60 g) sugar
1/2–1 tsp cinnamon powder
2.1 oz (60 g) raisins soaked in rum
juice from 1 lemon
3.5 oz (100 g) crumbled ladyfingers

For the pastry:

12 oz (350 g) strudel dough, home made (see above) or ready to prepare (cooling shelf)

Additional ingredients:

flour for the work surface
1.4 oz (40 g) melted butter for brushing · butter for the cookie sheet

8 to 10 servings

1 For the filling: Peel apples and slice down to the core. Alternatively, cut apples into quarters, peel, core and cut the quarters into 0.2 to 0.4 inch (5 to 10 mm) cubes. Brown the flaked almonds in a non-stick pan without fat. Mix sugar and cinnamon, add raisins, lemon juice, crumbled ladyfingers and browned almonds. Mix everything together with the apples.

2 For the pastry: Preheat the oven to 400 °F (200 °C). Sprinkle one of the balls of dough with flour and roll it out on a floured pastry cloth (about 16 x 16 inches / 40 x 40 cm) with a rolling pin. Carefully, pull the dough out over the back of the hand to a very thin rectangle and brush with melted butter immediately.

3 Spread half of the filling on the long side of the dough in a row. While doing so, leave a 2 inch (5 cm) border open on each of the narrow sides and wrap these towards the middle. Roll the strudel together with the help of the cloth. Place the strudel with the seam side down on a greased cookie sheet. Prepare the second strudel in the same way. Brush both strudels with melted butter and bake in the oven on the middle rack for about 20 to 25 minutes until golden brown.

4 Take the strudels out of the oven, leave to cool down and sprinkle with icing sugar before serving.

Caramelized Cherry Strudel

For the filling:

1.3 lb (600 g) cherries
1 fl oz (30 ml) cherry brandy
2 oz (50 g) hazel nuts
7 oz (200 g) ground almonds
0.8 oz (25 g) flour · 1 egg
2 oz (50 g) raw marzipan paste
2 oz (50 g) soft butter
2 oz (50 g) icing sugar
1/2 tsp grated zest each of organic lemon and orange
pulp from 1/2 vanilla pod
salt · cinnamon powder

For the pastry:

12 oz (350 g) strudel dough, home made (see left) or ready to prepare (cooling shelf)

Additional ingredients:

flour for sprinkling
2 oz (60 g) melted butter for brushing
butter for the cookie sheet
1.8 oz (50 g) icing sugar for sprinkling

8 to 10 servings

1 For the filling: Wash the cherries, pit and sprinkle with a few drops of cherry brandy. Preheat the oven to 400 °F (200 °C).

2 Chop hazel nuts coarsely and mix with almonds. Roast the mixture evenly on the cookie sheet in the oven on the middle rack for about 10 minutes until light brown, stirring from time to time. Remove from oven. Do not turn off the oven. Let the nuts and almonds cool off and mix them with flour.

3 Separate the egg. Blend the marzipan with the egg yolk until creamy. Mix the butter with icing sugar, lemon and orange zest, vanilla pulp, cinnamon powder and a pinch of salt until creamy. Add the creamy marzipan as well as the egg white and mix for a few minutes. Stir cherries and marzipan-butter paste into the nut-flour mixture.

4 For the pastry: Sprinkle one of the prepared balls of strudel dough with flour and roll it out on a pastry cloth (about 16 x 16 inches / 40 x 40 cm) with a rolling pin. Carefully, pull the dough out over the back of the hand to a very thin rectangle and brush with melted butter immediately.

5 Spread half of the filling on the long side of the dough in a row. While doing so, leave a 2 inch (5 cm) border open on each of the narrow sides and wrap these towards the middle. Roll the strudel together with the help of the cloth. Place the strudel with seam side down on a greased cookie sheet. Prepare the second strudel in the same way. Brush both strudels with melted butter and bake in the oven on the middle rack for about 20 to 25 minutes until golden brown.

6 Turn on the oven grill. Take the cherry strudel out of the oven and sprinkle it with a lot of icing sugar. Caramelize lightly under the preheated grill for 2 to 4 minutes.

"For chocolate cherry strudel, add 2.5 oz (70 g) of chopped dark chocolate couverture and 2.5 oz (70 g) of nougat pieces to the cherry filling. For an apricot strudel, substitute cherries and cherry brandy with apricots and apricot brandy "

MILLIRAHMSTRUDEL

For the filling:

4 oz (120 g) butter
1.4 oz (40 g) icing sugar
grated zest of 1 organic lemon and 1/2 organic orange
1 tbsp vanilla sugar
2 egg yolks
14 oz (400 g) farmer's cheese (quark), room temperature
1 1/4 cups (300 g) sour cream, room temperature
2 egg whites
1.8 oz (50 g) sugar · salt
0.8 oz (25 g) flour
2 oz (50 g) raisins, soaked in rum

For the pastry:

12 oz (350 g) strudel dough, home made (see page 166) or ready to prepare (cooling shelf)

Additional ingredients:

flour for sprinkling
1.8 oz (50 g) melted butter for brushing
butter for the roasting pan

For the eggmilk:

1 cup (250 ml) milk
1/4 cup (60 g) crème fraîche
2 eggs · 3 tbsp sugar
pulp from 1 vanilla pod

10 servings

1 For the filling: Whisk the butter with icing sugar, lemon and orange zest and the vanilla sugar in a bowl. Blend in the egg yolks, add farmer's cheese and sour cream a little at a time.

2 Whisk the egg white with a third of the sugar and a pinch of salt to form soft peaks, while trickling in the remaining sugar. Sift the flour into butter mixture and carefully fold in the drained raisins. Spoon the whisked egg whites under the batter.

3 For the pastry: Preheat the oven to 350 °F (180 °C). Cut each of the prepared balls of strudel dough in half. Sprinkle one half with flour and roll it out on a floured pastry cloth (about 16 x 16 inches / 40 x 40 cm) with a rolling pin. Carefully, pull the dough out over the back of the hand to a very thin rectangle and brush with melted butter immediately.

4 Spread a fourth of the filling on the long side of the dough in a row. While doing so, leave a 2 inch (5 cm) border open on each of the narrow sides and wrap these towards the middle. Roll the strudel together with the help of the cloth. Place the strudel with the seam side down in a greased roasting pan or a large oven dish (about 10 x 12 inches / 25 x 30 cm). Prepare the other three strudels in the same way. Place the strudels in the roasting pan. Brush all four strudels with melted butter and bake them in the oven on the middle rack for 15 minutes.

5 For the eggmilk: In the meantime, put milk with crème fraîche, eggs, sugar and vanilla pulp in a bowl. Mix with an electric mixer and pour through a sieve. Pour the eggmilk in the roasting pan and bake the strudels for another 30 minutes.

6 Remove the roasting pan from oven, allow the strudels to cool off in the pan for 20 minutes. To serve, cut the strudels into pieces. According to taste, sprinkle with icing sugar.

Alfons Schuhbeck

"A perfect side dish for the Millirahmstrudel – in Bavarian dialect, the name for cream strudel – is a fruity rhubarb compote, for instance."

Sweet Yeast Dumplings

For the dough:

1 cup (250 ml) milk
0.8 oz (25 g) yeast
1 oz (30 g) sugar
1.1 lb (500 g) flour
2 eggs · salt
2.8 oz (80 g) soft butter

Additional ingredients:

flour for the work surface
1 cup (250 ml) milk
0.7 oz (20 g) sugar
3 tbsp butter
1 oz (30 g) clarified butter or as a substitute ghee

6 servings

1 For the dough: Heat up the milk to lukewarm temperature. Add yeast and dissolve. Add two tablespoons of sugar. Put the flour in a bowl and make a well in the center. Pour the yeast milk in the well and mix with some flour. Cover the dough and leave to rise in a warm place for 15 minutes.

2 Whisk the eggs with a pinch of salt, add the remaining sugar and soft butter to the yeast sponge and then mix in flour. Knead the dough with a food processor or an electric mixer with dough hooks until the dough becomes smooth and elastic and separates from the bowl. Cover the dough again and leave to rise in a warm place for at least 45 minutes until it has doubled in volume.

3 Knead the dough with your hands firmly on a lightly floured work surface and then shape into rolls 1.6 to 3 inches (4 to 5 cm) in diameter. Cut the rolls into about 2 inch (5 cm) large pieces and shape every piece to a smooth ball.

4 Preheat the oven to 350 °F (180 °C). Warm the milk and sugar in a large low ovenproof saucepan (about 12 inches / 30 cm in diameter). Add the butter and the clarified butter to melt. Remove from stove. Place the balls of dough next to each other with the seam side down in the lukewarm milk. Cover the saucepan, and allow the sweet yeast dumplings to rise for 20 minutes. Cook the dumplings on top of the stove and over medium heat for 10 minutes.

5 Place the covered dish in the oven and bake the sweet yeast dumplings for about 35 minutes. Do not take off the lid in between, because the dumplings could collapse. If the crust at the bottom is still too light, place the saucepan back on top of the stove and cook over low heat until it is golden brown. Serve the sweet yeast dumplings while still warm. According to taste, they can also be served with vanilla sauce (see page 196, recipe “red berry compote with vanilla sauce”).

“For sweet yeast dumplings with apples, peel and core 1.1 lb (500 g) slightly sour apples and cut into pieces. Place the apple pieces in a saucepan with 1 oz (30 g) butter, 1 tablespoon vanilla sugar, 1 teaspoon lemon juice and 1 teaspoon cinnamon sugar. Place the balls of dough on top and bake as described above. Crust will not be formed, but the baked apples can be served as a side dish.”

Topfenpalatschinken

For the batter:

1 1/4 cup (300 ml) milk
2 tbsp sugar
a pinch of vanilla pulp
1/2 tsp grated zest each of organic lemon and orange
3.5 oz (100 g) flour · 4 eggs
3 tbsp brown butter (see page 26)

Additional ingredients:

2–3 tbsp butter for baking
1 tbsp butter for the pan

For the filling:

1.8 oz (50 g) soft butter
2 tbsp icing sugar
2 egg yolks
pulp from 1 vanilla pod
1/2 tsp grated organic lemon zest
10.5 oz (300 g) farmer's cheese (quark)
5/8 cup (150 g) cream
2 egg whites · salt
2.1 oz (60 g) sugar

For the eggmilk:

7 fl oz (200 ml) milk
2 eggs·1 tbsp sugar
1 tbsp vanilla sugar

4 servings

1 For the Palatschinken (pancake): Mix milk, sugar, vanilla pulp, lemon and orange zest in a bowl. Stir in the flour. First, mix in the eggs and then the brown butter with an electric mixer. Cover batter and leave to expand for about 30 minutes.

2 Pour the pancake batter through a sieve into a bowl. Melt some butter in a small skillet over medium heat and pour some batter into skillet with a ladle. Swinging the skillet a little bit left and right, fry the pancakes until golden brown on both sides. Fry seven more thin pancakes with the remaining batter in the same way.

3 For the filling: Beat butter with sifted icing sugar, egg yolks, vanilla pulp and lemon zest in a bowl until frothy and light colored. Blend the farmer's cheese (quark) and the cream into the butter mixture. First, beat egg whites with a pinch of salt and a third of the sugar until creamy, and then let the remaining sugar trickle in little by little and beat until stiff. Fold this mixture into the quark cream.

4 Preheat the oven to 350 °F (180 °C). Brush the pancakes with the quark cream, fold together, and fold the half circles into triangles. Grease an ovenproof dish with butter and layer the pancake triangles like roof shingles with the tips pointing into middle and towards the top of the dish.

5 For the eggmilk: Blend milk, eggs, sugar and vanilla sugar with an electric mixer and pour over the pancakes. Bake pancakes in the oven on the middle rack for 20 to 25 minutes until golden brown.

Alfons Schuhbeck

"The Topfenpalatschinken – in Bavaria (and Austria), the name for a rolled up pancake filled with quark – can be rolled in any preferred variation. The filling can be varied by adding raisins soaked in rum, apple cubes roasted in butter, blueberries or small cut apricots."

Dukatenbuchteln

For the dough:

3/4 cup (180 ml) milk
1 oz (30 g) yeast
1 lb (450 g) flour
2.6 oz (75 g) sugar
3 egg yolks
1 tsp almond liqueur, e.g. Amaretto
1 tbsp rum · salt
pulp from 1 vanilla pod
1 tsp grated zest each of organic lemon and orange
2.6 oz (75 g) soft butter

Additional ingredients:

flour for the work surface
butter for the dish
2 oz (60 g) melted butter for brushing
icing sugar for sprinkling

4 to 6 servings

1 For the dough: Heat up milk to lukewarm temperature. Crumble yeast with fingers and dissolve in milk. Knead the yeast milk together with flour, sugar, egg yolk, almond liqueur, rum, vanilla pulp, a pinch of salt as well as the lemon and orange zest. Add the butter and knead several minutes longer until the dough becomes smooth and elastic. Let the yeast dough sit in a bowl covered with plastic wrap for just under 30 minutes.

2 Knead the dough briefly once more and shape into a fat roll using flour as needed. Cut the roll into uniform slices and shape the slices into balls. Grease a roasting pan or an oven dish (about 8 to 12 inches / 20 x 30 cm) with butter. Place the dough balls inside, cover and leave to rise in a warm place for about 20 to 25 minutes.

3 Preheat the oven to 350 °F (180 °C). Brush the Dukatenbuchteln carefully with the melted butter and bake them in the oven on the lowest rack for about 20 minutes until golden brown.

4 Remove Dukatenbuchteln from oven and allow to cool off. Sprinkle the Buchteln with icing sugar and serve best with quince ragout (see page 194).

Alfons Schubbeck

"If you knead the yeast dough for the Dukatenbuchteln – in Bavaria, a special yeast cake with a very long tradition – one more time after it has already risen and then let it rise once more, the dough will have finer pores and will be more aromatic."

Topfen Dumplings

For the dumplings:

12 oz (350 g) farmer's cheese (quark)
3.5 oz (100 g) white bread
2 1/2 tbsp soft butter
2 tbsp icing sugar
a pinch of vanilla pulp
a pinch of grated organic lemon zest
salt · 1 egg yolk · 1 egg
5 oz (150 g) cinnamon crumbs

For the cooking water:

0.7 oz (20 g) salt
2.8 oz (80 g) sugar
1 scraped vanilla pod
2 slices ginger · 1/2 cinnamon bark
2 strips each of organic orange and lemon peel

4 servings

1 For the dumplings: Lay out a sieve with a wet cheesecloth and place the farmer's cheese inside. Using the cloth, press out as much fluid as needed to leave about 7 oz (200 g) of drained quark. Take the crust off the white bread and make crumbs in a food processor or a turbo blender.

2 Mix the butter with icing sugar, vanilla pulp, lemon zest and a pinch of salt in a bowl until creamy. Stir in egg yolk and egg. Add the quark (the Topfen) and the bread crumbs. Process all ingredients into a smooth mixture. Cover the quark mixture and refrigerate for about 30 minutes.

3 With wet hands, form eight dumplings of the same size from the quark mixture.

4 For the cooking water: Boil about 3 quarts (3 liters) water in a saucepan with salt and sugar. Add vanilla pod, ginger, cinnamon bark and lemon zest. Add the dumplings and simmer just below the boiling point for about 12 minutes. Remove the Topfen dumplings with a skimmer, drain on paper towel and coat them with cinnamon crumbs.

Topfen-Poppy Dumplings

Topfen dumplings (see above)
2 tbsp milk
1 tsp chopped dark chocolate couverture
0.8 oz (25 g) ground poppy seeds
1/2 tbsp sugar · 1/2 tsp honey
a few drops of rum
a pinch of vanilla pulp
0.7 oz (20 g) white bread crumbs

4 servings

1 Prepare Topfen dumplings as described above.

2 Heat up the milk and remove from stove. Add the couverture and melt. Mix in poppy seeds, sugar, honey, rum, vanilla pulp and white bread crumbs. Form eight small portions with a teaspoon and place them on a cookie sheet that is covered with parchment paper. Place the heaps in the freezer for 20 minutes until they have stiffened but are still malleable.

3 Roll the cold heaps with hands into balls and fill the dumplings with the poppy seed balls when shaping them.

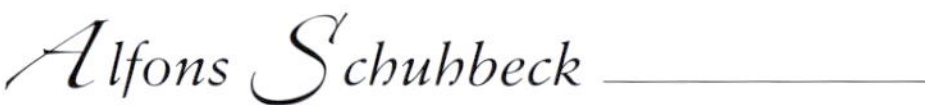

"For Topfen-Nougat Dumplings roll 2.8 oz (80 g) of nut nougats into eight balls of the same size with your hands. Put them in a cool place for at least 10 minutes. Fill the dumplings with the nougat balls when shaping them and complete as described above."

Caramelized Kaiserschmarren

For the Kasierschmarren:

4 oz (120 g) flour
1 cup (250 ml) milk
4 egg yolks
pulp from 1 vanilla pod
1 tsp grated organic lemon zest
1.4 oz (40 g) brown butter (see page 26)
4 egg whites · salt
2 oz (60 g) sugar
1.4 oz (40 g) butter
2–3 tbsp raisins, soaked in rum
2 tbsp flaked almonds (roasted)

Additional ingredients:

2 red apples
1 tbsp butter
1/2–1 tbsp sugar
1/3 cup (70 ml) dessert wine, e.g. Marsala or ice wine
icing sugar for sprinkling

4 servings

1 For the Kaiserschmarren: Blend flour and milk until smooth. Mix in egg yolks, vanilla pulp, lemon zest and brown butter. Beat egg whites with a pinch of salt until creamy. Let half of the sugar trickle in little by little and continue beating egg whites until stiff. Fold the beaten egg white into eggmilk.

2 Turn on the oven grill. Melt a teaspoon butter each in two small oven-proof pans (9 to 10 inches / 24 to 26 cm in diameter) over low heat on stove. Spread the Kaiserschmarren batter in the pan and brown the bottom lightly for about 2 minutes. Spread drained rum raisins and flaked almonds on top, taking care to cover the batter completely. Bake the Kaiserschmarren in pans one after another in the oven grill on the lowest rack for 3 minutes until golden brown.

3 Wash apples, quarter, core and cut the quarters into small wedges. Melt the butter and the sugar in a pan over medium heat. Add the apple wedges and braise lightly. Pour the dessert wine to the mixture and reduce almost completely.

4 Using two forks, shred the Kaiserschmarren into bite-size pieces. Stir in the one tablespoon of butter and the remaining sugar. While stirring and over medium heat, caramelize the Kaiserschmarren lightly. To serve, arrange the Kaiserschmarren on warmed plates with the braised apples and sprinkle with icing sugar.

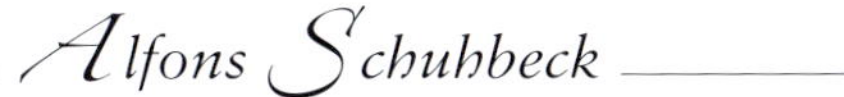

"For Apple-Walnut Kaiserschmarren: Peel three apples, cut in half and core. Cut the apple halves into small wedges and drizzle with a few drops of lemon juice. Brown briefly in a skillet on both sides with three tablespoons of butter and one tablespoon of sugar over medium heat. Dust with cinnamon powder and sprinkle three tablespoons of chopped walnuts on top. Shortly before serving, fold apple-nut mixture into Kaiserschmarren."

Yeast Plait

For the dough:

5/8 cup (150 ml) milk
0.7 oz (20 g) yeast
10 oz (300 g) flour
2 oz (50 g) sugar
2 egg yolks
1 tbsp almond liqueur, e.g. Amaretto
salt
a pinch of vanilla pulp
a pinch of grated organic lemon zest
1.8 oz (50 g) soft butter
2 tbsp raisins
1 tbsp rum

Additional ingredients:

melted butter and flour for the cookie sheet
1 egg

For the icing:

1.8 oz (50 g) icing sugar
1 tsp rum
1 tbsp flaked almonds

For about 1.1 lb (500 g)

1 For the dough: Heat up the milk to lukewarm temperature and pour into a bowl. Crumble yeast with fingers and dissolve in milk. Add flour, sugar, egg yolk, almond liqueur, a pinch of salt, vanilla pulp, and lemon zest and knead either with an electric mixer with dough hooks or a dough machine. Add the butter and knead the yeast dough until it is smooth and elastic and separates from the bowl.

2 Cover the dough and leave to rise in a warm place for about 30 minutes until his volume has doubled. Mix the raisins with the rum in a small bowl. Knead the dough for a few minutes, cover again and leave to rise for another 30 minutes.

3 Preheat the oven to 350 °F (180 °C). Brush the cookie sheet with melted butter and sprinkle with flour.

4 Drain the raisins and fold into dough. Knead the dough briefly one more time, and divide into three portions. Form three long strands and weave into a plait. Place the plait on a cookie sheet. Cover the plait and leave to rise in a warm place for 20 minutes.

5 Whisk egg and brush onto yeast plait. Bake the plait in the oven on the middle rack for 25 to 30 minutes until golden brown. Remove the plait from oven and allow to cool off completely.

6 For the icing: Mix the rum with a tablespoon of water. Toast the flaked almonds in a pan without fat. Brush the cooled off yeast plait with icing and sprinkle all over with the flaked almonds.

Alfons Schuhbeck

"The rum raisins have more flavor if they marinate in rum for one or two days. I always knead them into the dough at the end, so that they stay whole and do not discolor."

Christmas Stollen with Marzipan

For the fruit mixture:

3.5 oz (100 g) almonds, chopped and roasted
9 oz (250 g) currants
3.5 oz (100 g) raisins
2 oz (50 g) candied lemon peel, finely chopped
3.5 oz (100 g) candied orange peel, finely chopped
1/2 cup (120 ml) rum
2 drops bitter almond flavor
pulp from 1 vanilla bean
grated zest each of 1/2 organic lemon and orange

For the dough:

5/8 cup (150 ml milk)
3.2 oz (90 g) yeast
3 oz (80 g) honey
1.2 lb (520 g) flour (ideally Type 405)
10 oz (300 g) flour (ideally Type 550)
2 eggs · 2 egg yolks
14 oz (400 g) soft butter
flour for sprinkling
1 level tsp (6 g) salt

For the filling:

7 oz (200 g) raw marzipan paste
1 oz (30 g) icing sugar

Additional ingredients:

butter and flour for baking pan
9 oz (250 g) clarified butter or as a substitute ghee, melted
10 oz (300 g) vanilla sugar

For 2 stollens à about 2.9 lb (1.3 kg)

1 For the fruit mixture: A day in advance, mix almonds, currants, raisins, candied lemon and orange peel as well as rum, bitter almond flavor, vanilla pulp, grated lemon and orange zest in a bowl. Cover with plastic wrap and keep at room temperature.

2 For the dough: On the next day, heat up the milk to lukewarm temperature. Crumble yeast with fingers and dissolve in milk. Mix yeast milk with honey and 7 oz (200 g) flour (Type 405) until the dough has a stringy consistency. Cover the dough and leave to rise in a warm place for about 15 minutes.

3 Add the remaining flour, egg, egg yolk and 3.5 oz (100 g) butter to dough and knead either with an electric mixer with dough hooks or a dough machine. Knead the remaining butter little by little into the dough. Knead the yeast dough until it is smooth and forms bubbles. Sprinkle the dough with flour and cover with plastic wrap. Allow the dough to rise for 1 hour at room temperature until it has doubled in volume. Knead in gently the fruit mixture and the salt.

4 Grease two stollen baking pans with butter and dust with flour. Preheat the oven to 425 °F (220 °C). Form the dough into two fat, flat, oval shapes. Knead marzipan with icing sugar, mold into two rolls that are the same length as the flat dough shapes and insert into the middle of the stollen. Wrap the dough over the marzipan and roll up. Place the stollen dough with the seam side up in the pans and cover with the lid. Leave to rise for another 15 minutes.

5 Lower the oven temperature to 350 °F (175 °C). Bake the stollen on the middle rack for 50 to 60 minutes. Remove the Christmas stollen from baking pan. Allow the stollen to cool off a little and brush with clarified butter while still warm. Sprinkle with vanilla sugar and leave to cool off completely.

"You can make vanilla sugar yourself very easily: Infuse 10 oz (300 g) sugar with two scraped out vanilla pods in a jar with screw-top lid for 1 to 2 weeks. The stollen will be even tastier when 1/4 grated tonka bean is added. Grate this typical stollen spice like nutmeg. Stollen baked in a special baking pan is moister, but it can also be baked on a cookie sheet. In this case, place the shaped stollen seam side up on the cookie sheet."

Apfelkücherl

For the batter:

5.7 fl oz (170 ml) milk
3 tbsp butter · salt
3.5 oz (100 g) flour, sifted
3 eggs

Additional ingredients:

1 2/3 cups (400 ml) fat for frying
2.8 oz (80 g) sugar
1 1/2 tsp cinnamon powder
3 sour apples

For about 18 pieces

1 For the batter: Boil 2.4 fl oz (70 ml) milk with the same amount of water, the butter and a pinch of salt in a small saucepan. Pour the sifted flour into saucepan while stirring continually. Keep stirring the mixture for about 1 minute with a ladle until the batter separates from the bottom of the saucepan. Transfer the batter to a bowl and gradually stir in eggs and remaining milk until batter is thick.

2 Heat the fat to 350 °F (180 °C) in a deep skillet or deep-fat fryer. It is hot enough, when small bubbles form around the handle of a wooden spoon.

3 Mix the sugar with cinnamon powder. Peel apples, core with an apple corer and cut the apples crossways into 0.4 inch (1 cm) thick slices. Dip the slices in the batter, let excess drip off, and fry them for a few minutes until golden brown. Remove the Apfelkücherl with a skimmer, drain briefly on paper towel and immediately turn over in cinnamon sugar.

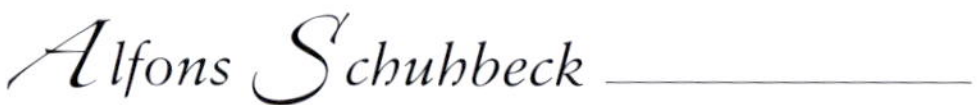

"The apple rings can be coated with wine or beer batter (see below) instead of choux pastry. In Bavaria, the name for this sort of apple pancakes is Apfelkücherl and the one for fried elderflowers is Hollerkücherl (see below)."

Hollerkücherl

For the batter:

7 oz (200 g) flour
1 1/4 cup (300 ml) white wine or beer
2 egg yolks
4 tbsp brown butter (see page 26)
a pinch of vanilla pulp
cinnamon powder
2 egg whites · salt
0.7 oz (20 g) sugar

Additional ingredients:

fat for frying · 2 oz (50 g) sugar
1/2 tsp cinnamon powder
12 elderflowers (umbels)

4 servings

1 For the batter: Mix the flour with the white wine in a bowl until smooth. Stir in egg yolks, brown butter, vanilla pulp and a pinch of cinnamon powder.

2 Whisk the egg whites with a pinch of salt and sugar until stiff and carefully blend into the wine dough.

3 Heat the fat to 350 °F (180 °C) in a large skillet or a deep-fat fryer. It is hot enough, when bubbles form around the handle of a wooden spoon.

4 Mix the sugar and the cinnamon powder on a plate. Pick through the elderflowers, dip them in batter, drain and fry until golden brown. Drain the Hollerkücherl briefly on paper towel and dip them immediately in cinnamon sugar.

Bavarian Doughnuts

1/2 cup (130 ml) milk
0.7 oz (20 g) yeast
1.6 oz (45 g) sugar
13 oz (375 g) flour
2 eggs · 2 egg yolks
pulp from 1/2 vanilla pod
1/2 tsp grated organic lemon zest
salt
1 tsp rum
4 1/2 tbsp soft butter
flour for the work surface
fat for frying
apricot or redcurrant jam
icing sugar for sprinkling

For about 10 pieces

1 Heat up the milk in a small saucepan until lukewarm (100 °F / 40 °C at the most). Crumble yeast with fingers, dissolve in milk and add a pinch of salt. Stir the yeast milk in a bowl with 5 oz (150 g) flour. Cover the dough with plastic wrap and leave to rise in a warm place for about 20 minutes.

2 Combine the remaining flour, sugar, eggs, egg yolks, vanilla pulp, lemon zest, a pinch of salt and the rum with the dough in a bowl of a dough machine and knead. Knead the butter little by little into the dough and knead for another 5 to 10 minutes until it is smooth and separates from the bowl. Cover the dough with plastic wrap and leave to rise at room temperature for about 25 minutes.

3 Knead the dough once more and leave to rise for another 15 minutes. Roll the dough to 1.2 inch (3 cm) thick rolls. Cut 0.6 to 0.8 inch (1 1/2 to 2 cm) thick slices from the rolls and roll them with your hands on the floured working surface to smooth balls. Place the balls with the seam down, about 2 inches (5 cm) apart, on a floured pastry cloth. Dust with some flour and allow the balls of dough to rise for 1 hour until its volume has increased about three quarters. Heat the fat to 325 °F (160 °C) in a large skillet or a deep-fat fryer.

4 Place the balls of dough with the smooth side down into the hot fat and fry them for 2 minutes with lid closed. Turn them with the help of two wooden spoon handles. Brown the bottom side of the balls, turn again and fry both sides each a little bit longer. Immerse the doughnuts briefly and remove them with a skimmer. Leave to drain on paper towel.

5 Fill the doughnuts with apricot or redcurrant jam with the help of a pastry bag and sprinkle icing sugar on top.

Alfons Schuhbeck

"For this sort of doughnuts – in Bavaria called Krapfen – you can use any other types of jam like rose hip or raspberry for filling. You can also use frosting instead of icing sugar."

Auszogne

For the dough:

1/2 cup (130 ml) milk
0.7 oz (20 g) yeast
13 oz (375 g) flour
1.4 oz (40 g) sugar
3 eggs · 2 egg yolks
pulp from 1/2 vanilla pod
1/2 tsp grated organic lemon zest
salt
3 tbsp soft butter

Additional ingredients:

flour for shaping
oil for cookie sheet, for brushing and for your hands
fat for frying
icing sugar for sprinkling

For about 12 pieces

1 For the dough: Heat up the milk until lukewarm. Crumble yeast with fingers and dissolve in the milk. Mix yeast milk with 5 oz (150 g) flour. Cover the dough with plastic wrap and leave to rise in a warm place for 20 minutes.

2 Knead the dough with the remaining flour, sugar, eggs, egg yolks, vanilla pulp, lemon zest and a pinch of salt either in a dough machine or with the dough hooks of an electric mixer. Knead the butter into the dough little by little and knead for another 5 to 10 minutes until it is smooth and separates from the bowl. Cover the dough with plastic wrap and leave to rise at room temperature for about 25 minutes.

3 Using some flour, shape twelve smooth balls of the same size from dough. Place the balls on a greased cookie sheet and brush them with oil. Cover the balls with plastic wrap and leave to rise in a warm place for 15 to 20 minutes until they have doubled in size.

4 Heat the fat to 325 °F (160 °C) in a large skillet or deep-fat fryer. Stretch the balls of dough carefully with lightly oiled hands until they are flat with a wide thick border and thin in the middle. Fry the Auszogne on both sides until golden brown. Remove with a skimmer and drain on paper towel. Sprinkle with icing sugar before serving.

French Toast

1/2 yeast plait from the day before or as an alternative 3 raisin bread rolls
3.5 oz (100 g) plum sauce
5 oz (150 g) sugar
1/4 – 1/2 tsp cinnamon powder
ground cloves
ground cardamom · 3 eggs
5 oz (150 g) milk
pulp from 1/2 vanilla pod
clarified butter or as an alternative ghee for deep-frying

4 servings

1 Cut the yeast plait into about 0.2 inch (5 mm) thick slices and brush half of the slices completely with plum sauce. Cover the brushed slices with the remaining slices.

2 Mix the sugar with cinnamon powder, a pinch each of ground cloves and ground cardamom in a deep plate.

3 Whisk eggs with milk and vanilla pulp. Heat the clarified butter in a pan. Dip the filled yeast plait slices briefly in the egg-milk mixture and fry in clarified butter over low heat on both sides until golden brown. Drain the French Tost (in Germany called Arme Ritter, pour knights) on paper towel and turn while still hot in the spice sugar. Serve on plates or on a platter.

Shortcrust Pastry (Basic Recipe)

6.2 oz (175 g) soft butter
2.6 oz (75 g) icing sugar
pulp from 1/2 vanilla pod
grated zest of 1/2 organic lemon
salt · 2 egg yolks
8.5 oz (240 g) flour

For about 1.1 lb (500 g)

1 Using a pastry blender or an electric mixer with dough hooks, combine butter, icing sugar, vanilla pulp, lemon zest and a pinch of salt in a bowl and blend until the dough is smooth. Add egg yolks one by one. Do not beat frothy.

2 Add the flour and knead only until the dough is smooth. Shape into flat rectangle, wrap in plastic wrap and refrigerate for at least 30 minutes.

3 Use the refrigerated dough according to the specific recipe.

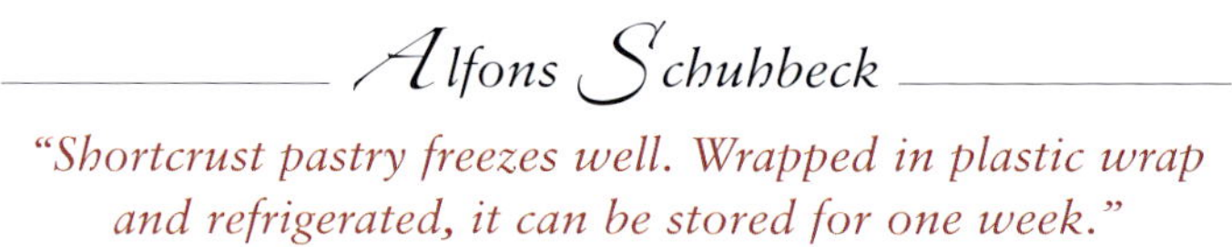

"Shortcrust pastry freezes well. Wrapped in plastic wrap and refrigerated, it can be stored for one week."

Cheese Cake with Apricots

For the dough:

1.6 lb (750 g) shortcrust pastry (see above)

For the topping:

2.2 lb (1 kg) farmer's cheese (quark)
7 oz (200 g) sugar
1/2 tsp grated organic lemon zest
1 tbsp vanilla sugar
salt · 3 eggs
5.6 oz (160 g) cream
1 oz (30 g) cornstarch
3.5 oz (100 g) almond slivers
9 oz (250 g) apricot jam

Additional ingredients:

flour for the work surface
fat for the cookie sheet

For 20 to 25 pieces

1 Prepare shortcrust pastry, wrap in plastic wrap and refrigerate for at least 30 minutes.

2 For the topping: Blend the farmer's cheese (quark) with sugar, lemon zest, vanilla sugar and a pinch of salt. Add the eggs and the cream. Mix in cornstarch and fold in almond slivers.

3 Wash apricots, cut in half, pit and cut into wedges. Preheat the oven to 400 °F (200 °C).

4 Briefly knead the shortcrust pastry one more time and roll out with a rolling pin on the lightly floured work surface until it is slightly larger than the cookie sheet. Place on the greased cookie sheet. Using a fork, poke holes into in the surface of the dough. Spread quark mixture over the dough and arrange apricots on top. Bake the cake in the oven on the lowest rack for about 50 minutes.

5 Heat up the apricot jam in a small saucepan and purée with a wand mixer. Brush the cake with jam and cut into rectangles.

Covered Apple Cake

For the dough:

1.6 lb (750 g) shortcrust pastry (see left)

For the filling:

2.2 lb (1 kg) apples
2 tbsp butter
3 tbsp sugar
1 tbsp vanilla sugar
1/2 tsp cinnamon powder
1/2 tsp grated organic lemon zest
1 tbsp lemon juice
2 oz (50 g) almond slivers
2 oz (50 g) raisins

Additional ingredients:

flour for the work surface
butter for the springform pan
4 tbsp biscuit crumbs, e.g. crumbled lady fingers or light sponge cake
1 small egg
2 tbsp cream

For 1 springform pan (10 inches / 26 cm diameter)

1 Prepare the shortcrust pastry, wrap in plastic wrap and refrigerate for at least 30 minutes.

2 For the filling: Peel the apples, core and cut into quarters. Cut the quarters into 0.4 to 0.6 inch (1 to 1 1/2 cm) cubes. Braise the apple dice in a deep skillet with butter, sugar, vanilla sugar, cinnamon powder and lemon zest for about 10 minutes. Add lemon juice, almond slivers and raisins. Allow the mixture to drain and cool off in a sieve.

3 Preheat the oven to 350 °F (180 °C). Briefly knead the shortcrust pastry one more time. Roll out one third of the dough on lightly floured work surface until it is 1.2 to 1.6 inches (3 to 4 mm) thick. Cut out a circle in the size of the springform pan. Place the dough circle on parchment paper. Using a fork, poke holes into the surface of the dough and transfer into the freezer compartment. Grease the springform pan with butter. Roll out the remaining dough 1.2 to 1.6 inches (3 to 4 mm) thick as well and cover bottom and sides of the springform pan. Sprinkle the dough with biscuit crumbs.

4 Mix the egg with the cream. Spread the drained apples on the dough. Fold the edges of dough over apples and brush with the egg-cream mixture. Remove the reserved dough circle from freezer and with the aid of the parchment paper, place on top of filling. Gently press on the edges. Brush with the remaining egg-cream mixture and bake in the oven on the lowest rack for about 1 hour until golden brown.

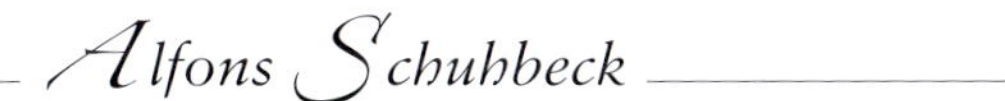

"The filling can be varied with pears: replace half of the apples with pears. The cake tastes best served lukewarm with softly whipped cream. I like to sprinkle a pinch of cinnamon powder on top of the cream."

ZWETSCHGENDATSCHI WITH STREUSEL TOPPING

For the dough:

1/2 cup (125 ml) milk
0.7 oz (20 g) yeast
10.5 oz (300 g) flour
1.8 oz (50 g) sugar · 2 egg yolks
1 tbsp almond liqueur, e.g. Amaretto
salt · a pinch of vanilla pulp
a pinch of grated organic lemon zest
1.8 oz (50 g) soft butter

Additional ingredients:

melted butter and flour for the cookie sheet
flour for the work surface

For the topping:

4.4 lb (2 kg) blue plums
2 oz (50 g) biscuit crumbs, e.g. crumbled lady fingers
2 oz (50 g) sugar
1/2 tsp cinnamon powder

For the streusel:

4.4 oz (125 g) flour
3 oz (90 g) sugar
1 tbsp vanilla sugar
3.5 oz (100 g) melted butter
salt · cinnamon powder
2.6 oz (75 g) flaked almonds

For 1 cookie sheet

1 For the dough: Warm up the milk until lukewarm (about 90 °F / 30 °C) in a small saucepan. Crumble yeast into milk and dissolve. Mix the yeast milk with flour, sugar, egg yolks, almond liqueur, a pinch of salt, vanilla pulp and lemon zest. Prepare the dough with your hands or using a food processor. Add the soft butter and knead for a few minutes until the dough is smooth and elastic.

2 Shape the dough into a ball, place in a bowl, cover with plastic wrap and leave to rise for about 30 minutes in a warm place.

3 Brush a cookie sheet with the melted butter and dust with flour. Roll out the dough into a thin layer and place on the cookie sheet. Using a fork, poke holes into the surface of the dough.

4 For the topping: Wash blue plums, cut in half and pit. Slice each of the plum halves lengthwise until the middle of the flesh. Spread biscuit crumbs over dough and cover tightly with the plum halves. Mix sugar and cinnamon powder in a small bowl and spread over the plums.

5 For the streusel: Using fingers, rub the flour, sugar, vanilla sugar, melted butter and a pinch of salt together to make crumbs. Loosely blend in the flaked almond. Spread streusel evenly over the Zwetschgendatschi. Leave to rise one more time for 20 minutes.

6 Preheat the oven to 350 °F (175 °C). Bake the Zwetschgendatschi in the oven on the middle rack for 30 to 40 minutes until golden brown. Remove from oven and leave to cool off. Cut cake into pieces. Serve with whipped cream according to taste.

"Zwetschgendatschi is the Bavarian name for this special sort of plum pie. Instead of yeast dough, you can use 1.6 lb (750 g) of shortcrust pastry. Roll out the pastry in size of the cookie sheet, place and prebake in the preheated oven (350 °F / 175 °C) for 8 to 10 minutes until light in color. Then proceed as above, covering the cake with plums."

SCHUHBECK'S BAVARIAN CREAM

2 leaves white gelatin
1 1/4 cups (300 g) cream
3 egg yolks
1.8 oz (50 g) icing sugar
pulp from 2 vanilla pods
1 tbsp cherry brandy

4 servings

1 Soak the gelatin in cold water. Whip the cream in a tall container with an electric mixer until it holds its shape softly (do not beat stiff). In a bowl, whisk egg yolks with the icing sugar and vanilla pulp until light and frothy.

2 Warm the cherry brandy in a small saucepan and remove from stove. Squeeze the gelatin well, dissolve in the cherry brandy while stirring and mix into the egg yolk mixture. Stir one third of the whipped cream into mixture, then carefully fold in the remaining whipped cream.

3 Pour the Bavarian cream into ramekins or dessert cups (volume about 4 fl oz / 120 ml). Refrigerate covered for about 2 hours until firm.

4 To serve, dip the ramekins until just below the rim in hot water for 7 to 8 seconds and turn over on a dessert plate. Serve with raspberry or strawberry sauce.

For almond brittle cream: Prepare a Bavarian cream as above, substituting the cherry brandy with almond liqueur, for instance Amaretto. Before refrigerating, fold brittle slivers into cream.

"It is easier to turn the cream over onto dessert plates if the molds are first dipped into hot water. Bring water to a boil in a small saucepan, immerse the mold until just below the rim (ceramic molds for about 8 seconds, metal molds only briefly) and turn the cream over onto a dessert plate."

Sour Cream Mousse

3 leaves white gelatin
13.5 oz (380 g) cream
6.3 oz (180 g) sour cream
juice from 2 lemons
1 tbsp icing sugar, sifted
1 tsp orange liqueur, e.g. Grand Marnier
1 tbsp vodka
1 egg white · 1 tbsp sugar

6 servings

1 Soak the gelatin in cold water. Blend 6.3 oz (180 g) cream with the sour cream, lemon juice and icing sugar in a bowl.

2 Warm up the orange liqueur and vodka in a small saucepan and remove from stove. Squeeze the gelatin well and dissolve while stirring in the liqueur-vodka mixture. Stir into sour cream mixture.

3 Whisk the egg white with the sugar until the mixture forms soft peaks. Whip the remaining cream until it softly holds its shape (do not beat stiff). Mix the beaten egg white with the cream just enough to blend and fold into the sour cream mixture. Fill the sour cream mousse into dessert molds (volume about 4 fl oz / 120 ml) and refrigerate covered for 2 hours.

Schuhbeck's Iced Coffee

For the coffee cream:

1 tbsp coffee beans
2 fl oz (50 g) cream
1 tsp sugar

For the coffee ice cream:

2 fl oz (50 ml) strong coffee, e.g. espresso
2 oz (50 g) sugar
2 egg yolks
1 tbsp rum
3.4 fl oz (100 g) cream

Additional ingredients:

ground cardamom

4 servings

1 For the coffee cream: A day in advance toast the coffee beans in a non-stick skillet without fat over low heat until fragrant. Place into a bowl and mix with the cream and the sugar. Cover and leave to infuse for about 1 day in the refrigerator.

2 For the coffee ice cream: In a small saucepan, heat up the coffee with half of the sugar until the sugar is dissolved.

3 Beat the egg yolks with the remaining sugar until frothy. Slowly stir in the coffee and beat the mixture in a double boiler or a metal bowl immersed in hot water to fine foam. Temperature of egg yolk mixture should not exceed 175 °F (80 °C). Beat the mixture until cold, using a food processor or filling the bottom of the double boiler with ice water. Add the rum. Beat the cream until it softly holds its shape and fold into coffee foam.

4 Fill the coffee foam into coffee cups up to 0.6 inch (1 1/2 cm) below the rim. Freeze in freezer compartment for about 2 hours.

5 To prepare for serving, strain the prepared coffee cream through a sieve and whip until it softly holds its shape. Place small dollops of coffee cream on top of the frozen coffee ice cream and dust with a pinch of cardamom. Before serving, place cups into refrigerator for 20 to 30 minutes to obtain the desired temperature for ice cream.

Semolina Flummery

2 egg yolks
4 tbsp sugar
3 leaves white gelatin
1/2 vanilla pod
1 cup (250 ml) milk
a pinch grated zest each of organic lemon and orange
a pinch freshly grated ginger
1.4 oz (40 g) durum wheat semolina
1 tsp rum
1 tbsp orange liqueur, e.g. Grand Marnier
1 egg white · salt
7 fl oz (200 g) cream

4 servings

1 Beat the egg yolks with a tablespoon sugar in a bowl until light and frothy. Soak the gelatin in cold water.

2 Slice the vanilla pod open lengthwise. In a saucepan, bring the milk to a boil with two tablespoons of sugar, lemon and orange zest as well as vanilla pod and ginger. Trickle in semolina while stirring. Cook to porridge over low heat for 3 to 5 minutes while stirring continually. Remove from stove and take out the vanilla pod.

3 Stir the semolina porridge portionwise into the egg yolk mixture. Squeeze the gelatin well and dissolve in the warm semolina mixture. Stir in the rum and orange liqueur and allow the mixture to cool down to room temperature.

4 Beat the egg white with a pinch of salt and the remaining sugar until it forms soft peaks. Whip cream until it softly holds its shape. Mix egg white with cream just enough to blend and fold into semolina mixture.

5 Fill the semolina mixture into dessert molds (volume about 4 fl oz / 120 ml), cover and refrigerate for 2 hours.

6 To serve, dip the molds 7 to 8 seconds up to rim in hot water and turn the semolina flummery over on dessert plates. Garnish with chocolate curls or lemon balm leaves to taste. Serve Apricot Roester (see page 195) with the semolina flummery.

"Ginger contains enzymes which prevent gelatin from setting. Since these enzymes are destroyed by heat, ginger should be cooked together with the liquid."

White Chocolate Mousse

2 leaves white gelatin
7 oz (200 g) white chocolate couverture
13 fl oz (380 g) cream
3 egg yolks
1 tsp sugar
3 tbsp cherry brandy

4 servings

1 Soak the gelatin in cold water. Finely chop the couverture, place with 1/4 cup (80 g) cream into a metal bowl or a double boiler and melt while stirring.

2 Beat the egg yolks with the sugar in a bowl with a wire whisk until light and frothy. Stir in the couverture-cream mixture. Heat up the cherry brandy in a small saucepan and remove from stove. Squeeze the gelatin well and dissolve, while stirring, in cherry brandy. Stir into the chocolate cream and allow to cool off.

3 Whip the remaining cream until it softly holds its shape. Stir one third of the cream with the wire whisk into chocolate cream. Carefully fold in the remaining two thirds of whipped cream. Pour the white chocolate mousse into a bowl, cover and refrigerate for 2 hours.

4 To serve, use an ice cream scoop or a table spoon to spoon out balls of mousse, dipping spoon or scoop into hot water from time to time. Arrange on dessert plates with brandied cherries or raspberry sauce.

Dark Chocolate Mousse

6.3 oz (180 g) dark chocolate couverture
1 small egg
1 egg yolk
1–2 tsp rum
1–2 tsp brandy
1 2/3 cups (400 g) cream

4 servings

1 Chop the couverture coarsely and melt in a double boiler or a metal bowl immersed in hot water while stirring.

2 Beat the egg and the egg yolk in a metal bowl immersed in hot water until light and frothy. Stir in the melted couverture. Fold in the rum and the brandy and allow mixture to cool off.

3 Whip the cream until it softly holds its shape and fold into chocolate cream. Fill the mousse into a bowl, cover and refrigerate for 2 hours

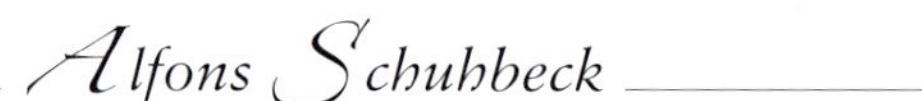

"To prepare chocolate mousse from milk chocolate, use 1.8 oz (50 g) milk chocolate couverture and 4.6 oz (130 g) dark chocolate couverture. Rum can be substituted with Pear brandy. For a firm mousse, soak two leaves of white gelatine, squeeze and dissolve in the warm pear brandy before mixing into chocolate cream."

Frozen Kaiserschmarren

For the parfait:

2 egg yolks · 1 egg
2 oz (60 g) sugar
pulp from 1 vanilla pod
a pinch of grated organic lemon zest
7 fl oz (200 g) cream
1.4 oz (40 g) rum raisins
oil for the dish

For the icing:

3.5 oz (100 g) milk chocolate
3 tbsp oil

Additional ingredients:

1 tbsp flaked almonds

Für 4 Personen

1 For the parfait: In a metal bowl, beat egg yolks and egg with one third of the sugar, vanilla pulp and lemon juice until light and frothy.

2 In a small saucepan, simmer 2 1/2 tablespoons of water with the remaining sugar over low heat for 1 minute. Stir the sugar syrup into the egg foam and beat the mixture in a double boiler to fine foam, not exceeding 180 °F (85 °C). Fill the bottom of the double boiler with ice water and beat the foamy egg mixture until cold (or use a food processor).

3 Whip the cream until it softly holds its shape and fold under the cold egg foam together with the rum raisins. Grease an ovenproof dish and cover with parchment paper. Spread out the parfait mixture 0.4 inch (1 cm) thick and freeze 2 to 3 hours in the freezer compartment.

4 For the icing: Coarsely chop the milk chocolate and melt the pieces in a double boiler while stirring. Stir in oil. Remove the parfait from freezer and brush with a thin layer of the melted chocolate. Return to freezer compartment for another 10 minutes.

5 Toast the flaked almonds in a non-stick pan without fat and leave to cool off. Coarsely break up the parfait like a typical Kaiserschmarren, arrange on cooled plates and sprinkle with the toasted almonds.

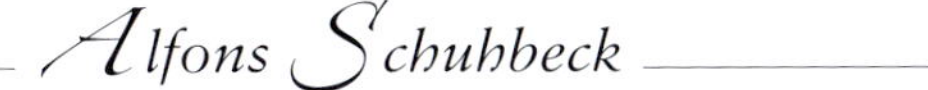

"It is best to break the frozen Kaiserschmarren into pieces using fingers. For hygienic purposes, use disposable gloves. In a suitable container frozen Kaiserschmarren can be stored in the freezer compartment for 2 days. This dessert can be served all year round because it harmonizes well with all kinds of seasonal fruit, from cherries to berries, Apricot Roester (see page 195), elderberry compote or brandied quince."

Elderflower Sorbet

4.2 oz (120 g) elderflowers, picked fresh, without stems
1 1/4 cup (300 ml) dry white wine
7 fl oz (200 ml) sparkling wine
7.8 oz (220 g) sugar
1 clove
juice from 2 lemons

4 servings

1 A day in advance, pick through the elderflowers thoroughly and fill into a large jug.

2 In a saucepan, bring the white wine with 7 fl oz (200 ml) water, sparkling wine, sugar, clove and lemon juice to a boil and simmer until sugar has dissolved. Allow the wine syrup to cool off.

3 Pour the warm syrup on top of the elderflowers in the jug. Cover the mixture with paper towel, letting the paper float on top of the liquid. Allow the elderflower brew to infuse at least 1 day in the fridge.

4 Remove the elderflower brew from fridge and strain through a fine sieve into a bowl. Freeze brew until creamy in the ice cream maker. Pour into a freezer-safe ice cold bowl or into freezer-safe glasses and store covered in the freezer compartment until ready to serve.

5 Serve the elderflower sorbet with frozen elderflower umbels and small wafer rolls as desired. The elderflower sorbet can be stored in the freezer compartment for about 1 day.

For strawberries in elderflower jelly: Wash a few strawberries, clean and cut into quarters or eighths and distribute in glasses. Slightly warm up 1 2/3 cups (400 ml) elderflower brew. Soak three leaves white gelatin, squeeze well, dissolve in the elderflower brew and pour lukewarm on top of the strawberries.

"For a refreshing summer aperitif, I like to fill some elderflower sorbet into champagne glasses and top with sparkling wine. Elderflower brew can also be used to marinate fruit salads or as a basic ingredient for a glaze on top of raspberry cake."

Elderberry-Pear Ragout

7 oz (200 g) elderberries
1 tbsp cornstarch
1 1/4 cups (300 ml) strong red wine
2 oz (60 g) sugar
1/2 vanilla pod
1 strip each of organic lemon and orange peel
0.8 inch (2 cm) cinnamon bark
2 pears, about 12 oz (350 g)
1 tsp lemon juice

4 servings

1 Pick through the elderberries and wash. Dissolve cornstarch in two tablespoons of red wine and stir until smooth. Caramelize half of the sugar in a saucepan. Deglaze the caramel with the remaning red wine and reduce the red wine brew by one third.

2 Stir the dissolved cornstarch into the red wine brew and simmer over low heat for 2 to 3 minutes. Slice the vanilla pod open lengthwise and add to saucepan together with lemon and orange peel, cinnamon bark and the elderberries. Allow the ragout to infuse just below the boiling point for 5 minutes.

3 In the meantime, peel the pears, quarter and core. Cut the quarters into small wedges. Add the pear wedges to the elderberry ragout and steam together over low heat for 3 minutes.

4 Remove the elderberry-pear ragout from stove, season with lemon juice and leave to cool off. Remove all spices. The ragout is excellent with Dukatenbuchteln (see page 172).

Quince Ragout

3 oz (80 g) sugar
1 tbsp lemon juice
4 tbsp orange juice
5/8 cup (150 ml) dry white wine
2 fl oz (50 ml) white port wine
5/8 cup (150 ml) Prosecco or dry sparkling wine
1/4 cinnamon bark
pulp from 1/2 vanilla pod
1 strip each of organic lemon and orange peel
2 large quince
0.7 oz (20 g) cornstarch

4 servings

1 Caramelize the sugar in a saucepan over medium heat until golden brown. Deglaze with lemon and orange juice. Add white wine, port wine, Prosecco or sparkling wine, cinnamon bark, vanilla pulp and lemon and orange peel. Simmer for a few minutes over low heat until the caramel has dissolved. Remove from stove.

2 Peel the quinces, cut into quarters and core. Cut the quarters into 0.4 inch (1 cm) cubes. Add the quince cubes to caramel brew and simmer over low heat for about 15 minutes until soft. Strain through a sieve into a saucepan and remove spices again.

3 Bring the quince-caramel brew to a boil. Dissolve the cornstarch in a little bit cold water and stir until smooth. Add to brew while stirring continually and simmer over low heat for 2 minutes. Add the strained quinces and stir. Allow quince ragout to cool off. It is an excellent accompaniment for Kaiserschmarren (see page 175) and Dukatenbuchteln (see page 172).

Apricot Roester

2.2 lb (1 kg) apricots
5 oz (150 g) sugar
juice from 1 lemon
1 cinnamon bark
1/2 vanilla pod

4 servings

1 Wash apricots, cut in half and pit. Cut the halves into quarters. Mix the apricot quarters with sugar, lemon juice, cinnamon bark and vanilla pod, spread on a cookie sheet, cover and leave to infuse for 30 minutes. Preheat the oven to 350 °F (180 °C).

2 Cook the apricots in the oven on the middle rack for 12 to 15 minutes until soft, stirring from time to time. Remove the apricot roester from oven and cool off until lukewarm. Remove cinnamon bark and vanilla pod.

Blue Plum Roester

1.1 lb (500 g) blue plums
about 2.5 oz (70 g) sugar
juice from 1/2 lemon
1/2 cinnamon bark
1/2 vanilla pod
2 fl oz (50 ml) strong red wine
1 fl oz (30 ml) port wine
1 tsp cornstarch

4 servings

1 Preheat the oven to 350 °F (180 °C). Wash plums, cut in half and pit. Cut the halves into quarters. In an ovenproof dish, mix plum quarters with sugar, lemon juice, cinnamon bark and vanilla pod. Add the red wine and the port wine.

2 Cook the plums in the oven on the middle rack for 15 to 20 minutes until not too soft, stirring from time to time. Remove the blue plum roester from oven and remove cinnamon bark and vanilla pod. Strain the wine brew through a sieve into a small saucepan. Return the plums to the ovenproof dish.

3 Dissolve the cornstarch in a little bit cold water and stir until smooth. Bring the wine brew to a boil, stir in the cornstarch and gently simmer for 2 minutes. Pour the brew on top of plums, cover and leave to infuse for several hours.

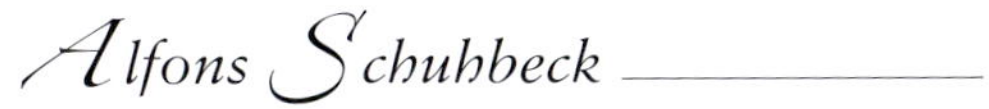

"The riper and hence the sweeter the fruit, the less sugar you will need for the Roester (a Bavarian specialty, composed of flavored fruits baked in the oven). For a plum roester without alcohol, prepare plums as described, mix 2 oz (60 g) sugar with 1/2 teaspoon of cinnamon powder, sprinkle on top of the plums and leave to infuse for 20 minutes. Cook the plum roester on a cookie sheet in the oven (preheated to 350 °F / 180 °C) for 15 to 20 minutes, stirring from time to time."

Red Berry Compote with Vanilla Sauce

For the compote:

2 tsp cornstarch
5/8 cup (150 ml) black currant juice
3.4 fl oz (100 ml) cherry juice
2 tbsp sugar
1/2 vanilla pod
1 sliver of cinnamon bark
1 slice ginger
1 strip organic orange peel
1.4 fl oz (40 ml) Cassis liqueur
1.1 lb (500 g) mixed berries, e.g. red and black currants, blueberries, raspberries, gooseberries, strawberries

For the vanilla cream:

1/2 vanilla pod
7 fl oz (200 g) cream
2 tbsp icing sugar

Für 4 Personen

1 For the compote: Dissolve cornstarch in three tablespoons of blackcurrant juice and stir until smooth. In a saucepan, bring the remaining blackcurrant juice, the cherry juice and the sugar to a boil. Stir in the dissolved cornstarch and simmer over low heat for 2 minutes. Remove saucepan from stove.

2 Add vanilla pod, cinnamon bark, ginger and orange peel to the juice mixture and stir in Cassis liqueur. Allow the spices to infuse for 10 minutes.

3 Pick through the red and black currants, blueberries, raspberries and gooseberries and wash. Wash the strawberries, clean and depending on size, cut into quarters or eighths.

4 Pour the juice mixture through a sieve into a bowl. Add the berries and leave to infuse for 20 minutes.

5 For the vanilla cream: Slice the vanilla pod open lengthwise and scrape out pulp. Whip cream with icing sugar until it holds its shape softly, stirring in the vanilla pulp.

6 Serve the red berry compote with vanilla cream and garnish with berries dipped in sugar according to taste.

"Pitted cherries can also be added to the berry mixture. Out of season, frozen berries can be used. In this case, pour the boiling hot juice mixture on top of the frozen berries and remove the spices after 20 minutes.
The vanilla cream has many possible variations. For rum cream, substitute the vanilla pulp with one tablespoon of rum. For orange cream, instead of vanilla pulp, stir some orange liqueur (e.g. Grand Marnier) and a pinch of grated organic orange zest into the cream."

P

R

S

W

PICTURE CREDITS

Susie Eising: page 9 (above left)
Helmut Henkensiefken: page 15 (above)

Are you in the mood to cook and more?

Alfons Schuhbeck's highly rated restaurant "Südtiroler Stuben", his wine bistro, his ice cream parlor and his spice shop are located at "Am Platzl", the famous square in Munich. Here you will find everything your culinary heart desires. "Am Platzl" is also home to Schuhbeck's cooking school.

For more information on the Internet, by phone or in person:
Schuhbeck's
Am Platzl
D-80331 München
Phone: +49(0)892166900
or www.schuhbeck.de